CONTENTS

1. THE FIRST STEPS

Everyone familiar with the **Old Testament** will know that genealogies are among the oldest writings of the Hebrews. The Greeks and other ancient races also valued records of descent. In modern times there has been a revival of interest, and genealogy has become almost as popular as stamp and coin collecting; but some people do not know how or where to begin. The purpose of this little book is to guide the beginner in his or her search for Scottish ancestry.

Initially, it is best to do your own spadework, and the home is the best place to begin. It is often surprising how much information can be gleaned from family sources, which, apart from old bibles, may include:

Degrees	Heirlooms
Diplomas	Portraits
Schools reports	Photographs
Testimonials	Silverware
References	Samplers
Service discharge papers	Marriage records
Medals	Baptismal certificates
Seals	Funeral records
Letters	Telegrams
Journals	Scrapbooks
Newspaper cuttings	Postcard albums
Diaries	Insurance records
Rent books or leases	Property deeds
Bookplates	Naturalisation papers

In every family there is usually one member--a parent or perhaps a maiden great-aunt--who has preserved items such as those listed. Some elderly people are suspicious of such modern inventions as tape-recorders and even telephones, so inquiries should be conducted with care. A personal visit is best, and the production of family photographs is fairly easy to encourage. You can then seek to identify people. Ask if you can take a few notes and commence gathering details. Four "keys" which unlock many doors are NAME, RELATIONSHIP, DATE and PLACE.

Having made a good beginning you can now approach relatives who may not be so well versed in the family history, but who may possess valuable pieces of information. You can ask about childhood memories, especially about ancestors and relatives; school and/or college days; scholastic and sports achievements; occupation or profession.

Most people associate dates with events, and like a good detective
you can ask questions which lead to the elucidation of pertinent
facts. "Did grandmother die before the family moved to New England?"
"Was Uncle Bill too young to serve in World War II?" "I expect John
had emigrated before Marilyn got married?" The answers to questions
like these can narrow down time periods and save expense when you come
to search among "official" records.

If relatives live a long distance away, you can write to them,
being sure to enclose a self-addressed return envelope. International
Reply Coupons are useful if they live in another country. Some
genealogists devise elaborate questionaires, but our advice is to
restrict your first inquiries to a few easily answered questions.
"What were the names of your parents?" "When and where were they
born?" "Do you remember your grand-parents?" Too many questions to a
busy person may result in lack of co-operation. Always acknowledge a
reply. When you write again asking further questions you can give
something in return. A draft genealogical chart can work wonders.

In your enthusiasm do not try to invent a new form of shorthand.
Write clearly, and do not use scraps of paper which can be mislaid or
lost. Obtain a strong pad of opaque notepaper, large enough to tabu-
late fragments of pedigree and see relationships at a glance.

Now that you are almost ready to visit court-houses or record offices, you may wish to decide on some method of charting the family.
The numbered genealogy chart so popular in the U.S.A. is useful as you
can plot your way backwards with the basic details before you. No. 1
can be either male or female, after which the males have even numbers
and the females odd numbers. This type of chart covers the ground
back to your great-great-grandparents, whose numbers can be carried
over to a fresh chart. Used in conjunction with family group sheets,
these can be secured in ring binders or special **Book of Remembrance**
folders. One advantage of the groupsheet is that naming patterns can
be easily compared.

Avoid fancy charts with tree trunks, branches and foliage; or
"wheel" or "fan" type charts. The conventional "drop-line" chart is
much better for illustration or display, but not so easy to manage. A
simple example is shown in the center pages of this book, and more
extensive charts can be drawn with practice. The knack is to keep the
main line of the family on the left side of the chart coming down
ahead of the people to be shown under the horizontal lines further
right, and then space out the siblings to give the chart some balance.

HUSBAND DONALD WHYTE

			Place
Born	13. 12. 1811		Kilmun, Argyll
Chr.	15. 12. 1811		do.
Marr.		1842	do.
Died	9. 5. 1879		Galashiels, Selkirkshire
Bur.	5. 1879		Gladhouse, Selkirkshire

HUSBAND'S FATHER — Donald Whyte
HUSBAND'S OTHER WIVES

WIFE MARY MOFFAT

			Place
Born		1823	Morton, Roxburghshire
Chr.		1823	do.
Died	9. 12. 1889		Sydney, Australia
Bur.	12. 1889		do.

WIFE'S FATHER — John Moffat
WIFE'S MOTHER — Mary Thomson
WIFE'S OTHER HUSBANDS

SEX M/F	CHILDREN List Each Child (Whether Living or Dead) in Order of Birth SURNAME (CAPITALISED) GIVEN NAMES	WHEN BORN DAY MONTH YEAR	WHERE BORN TOWN	COUNTY	STATE OR COUNTRY	DATE OF FIRST MARRIAGE TO WHOM	WHEN DIED DAY MONTH YEAR
1	JOHN	15. 3. 1843	Kilmun	Argyll Scot.		26. 6. 1874 JANE SPIERS	18. 1. 1920
2	DONALD	6. 4. 1845	Blairmore	do.	do.	16. 7. 1873 AGNES MURRAY	28. 4. 1880
3	MARY	6. 7. 1847	do.	do.	do.	-unm.-	6. 7. 1847
4	ANN twin	6. 7. 1847	do.	do.	do.	-unm.-	13. 9. 1865
5	EUPHEMIA	13. 10. 1849	do.	do.	do.	21. 12. 1877 JAMES JACKSON	
6	CHRISTINE	21. 12. 1851	do.	do.	do.	27. 7. 1867	
7	VIOLET	18. 1. 1855	Laidlawkiel, Stow	Mid Lothian	do.	-unm.-	2. 10. 1875
8	ISOBELLA	13. 3. 1857	do.	do.	do.	29. 6. 1882 JAMES HENRY MURRAY	
9							
10							
11							

SOURCES OF INFORMATION
Old Parochial Register of Dunoon & Kilmun
510/2, & statutory registers.

American ancestry of
Sir WINSTON S. CHURCHILL
1874-1965

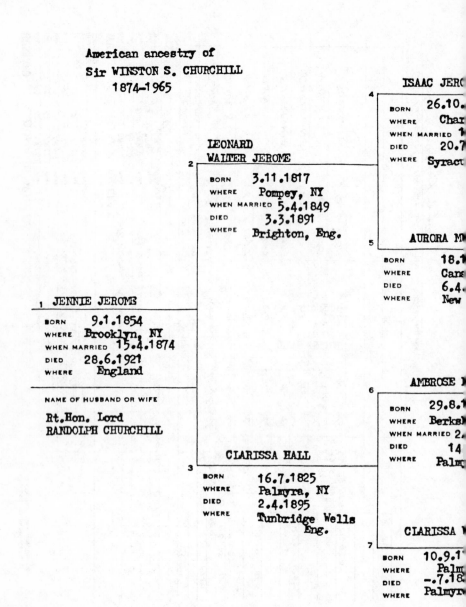

4 ISAAC JER(
BORN   26.10.
WHERE   Char
WHEN MARRIED 1
DIED   20.7
WHERE   Syracu

2 LEONARD
WALTER JEROME
BORN   3.11.1817
WHERE   Pompey, NY
WHEN MARRIED 5.4.1849
DIED   3.3.1891
WHERE   Brighton, Eng.

5 AURORA M
BORN   18.1
WHERE   Can
DIED   6.4.
WHERE   New

1 JENNIE JEROME
BORN   9.1.1854
WHERE   Brooklyn, NY
WHEN MARRIED 15.4.1874
DIED   28.6.1921
WHERE   England

NAME OF HUSBAND OR WIFE
Rt.Hon. Lord
RANDOLPH CHURCHILL

6 AMBROSE
BORN   29.8.
WHERE   Berks
WHEN MARRIED 2.
DIED   14
WHERE   Palm

3 CLARISSA HALL
BORN   16.7.1825
WHERE   Palmyra, NY
DIED   2.4.1895
WHERE   Tunbridge Wells
         Eng.

7 CLARISSA
BORN   10.9.1
WHERE   Palm
DIED   -.7.18
WHERE   Palmyr

PEDIGREE CHARTS
available from
THE SCOTTISH GENEALOGY SOCIETY

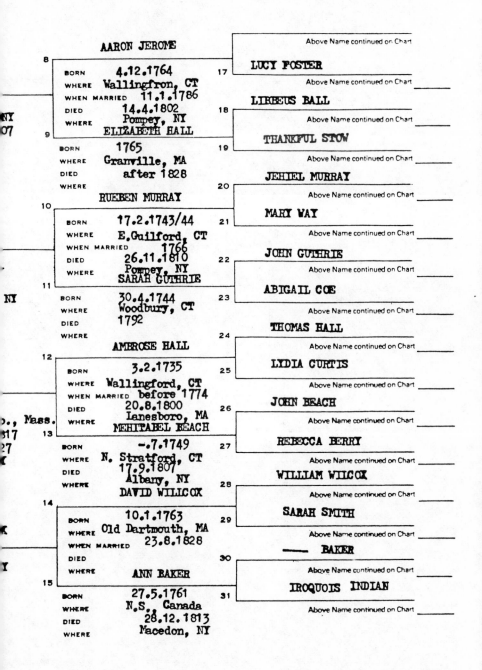

8 **AARON JEROME**

BORN	4.12.1764
WHERE	Wallingfron, CT
WHEN MARRIED	11.1.1786
DIED	14.4.1802
WHERE	Pompey, NY

9 **ELIZABETH HALL**

BORN	1765
WHERE	Granville, MA
DIED	after 1828
WHERE	

10 **RUEBEN MURRAY**

BORN	17.2.1743/44
WHERE	E.Guilford, CT
WHEN MARRIED	1766
DIED	26.11.1810
WHERE	Pompey, NY

11 **SARAH GUTHRIE**

BORN	30.4.1744
WHERE	Woodbury, CT
DIED	1792
WHERE	

12 **AMBROSE HALL**

BORN	3.2.1735
WHERE	Wallingford, CT
WHEN MARRIED	before 1774
DIED	20.8.1800
WHERE	Lanesboro, MA

13 **MEHITABEL BEACH**

BORN	-.7.1749
WHERE	N. Stratford, CT
DIED	17.9.1807
WHERE	Albany, NY

14 **DAVID WILLCOX**

BORN	10.1.1763
WHERE	Old Dartmouth, MA
WHEN MARRIED	23.8.1828
DIED	
WHERE	

15 **ANN BAKER**

BORN	27.5.1761
WHERE	N.S., Canada
DIED	28.12.1813
WHERE	Macedon, NY

17 LUCY FOSTER *Above Name continued on Chart* ____

Above Name continued on Chart ____

18 LIBBEUS BALL *Above Name continued on Chart* ____

19 THANKFUL STOW *Above Name continued on Chart* ____

20 JEHIEL MURRAY *Above Name continued on Chart* ____

21 MARY WAY *Above Name continued on Chart* ____

22 JOHN GUTHRIE *Above Name continued on Chart* ____

23 ABIGAIL COE *Above Name continued on Chart* ____

24 THOMAS HALL *Above Name continued on Chart* ____

25 LYDIA CURTIS *Above Name continued on Chart* ____

26 JOHN BEACH *Above Name continued on Chart* ____

27 REBECCA BERRY *Above Name continued on Chart* ____

28 WILLIAM WILCOX *Above Name continued on Chart* ____

29 SARAH SMITH *Above Name continued on Chart* ____

30 —— BAKER *Above Name continued on Chart* ____

31 IROQUOIS INDIAN *Above Name continued on Chart* ____

If you can make a fair shape at drawing this kind of chart, you may wish to send copies to friends and relatives. The cheapest method of production is make a pencil draft, then draw the chart on good tracing paper with black ink. This will act as a negative and you can have prints run off at a copying office.

Genealogical studies cannot be pursued in splendid isolation, and it is worthwhile joining a local genealogical society. Other members can share their knowledge with you, and such organisations usually publish or circulate newsletters or magazines, and run courses on genealogy. Wherever you are, you would benefit from membership of the Scottish Genealogy Society. This society cannot undertake research for you, but its quarterly journal, **The Scottish Genealogist**, is invaluable. It also publishes volumes of gravestone inscriptions, genealogy charts, family group sheets and census worksheets, at reduced rates to members. Applications for membership should be addressed to:

> The Membership Secretary,
> Scottish Genealogy Society,
> 9 Union Street,
> Edinburgh, Scotland, EH1 3LT

A visit to cemeteries or family burial plots may furnish genealogical details from tombstones or grave-markers. The next step is to find out what genealogical material is available at your local library. You should also learn what categories of records are preserved in your city, county or state record office, or regional, provincial or university archives.

If you live outside Scotland you must try to get back to your immigrant ancestor. Should family sources prove who he was, you might be fortunate enough to find his time of arrival from a passenger list. For published lists relating to the U.S.A. and Canada, P.W. Filby's encyclopaedic **Bibliography of Ship Passenger Lists**, 1538-1900, published by Gale Research Co., Detroit, is indispensable, and may be used in conjunction with the three-volume **Passenger and Immigration Lists Index**, published by the same firm. An updated edition of the **Bibliography** will include recent works such as David Dobson's **Directory of Scottish Settlers in North America**, 1625-1825 (Baltimore, 1984).

There is still umpublished immigration material in libraries and archives. For the U.S.A. data of this kind are mainly in the National

Archives; for Canada in the Public Archives, at Ottawa, and in some
provincial repositories. The best source for Australia is probably
the National Library, at Canberra.   For New Zealand there are
shipping lists in the Alexander Turnbull Library in Wellington. The
records of the New Zealand Land Co. are in the Nelson Provincial
Museum.

The bulk of "official" Scottish records are centralised in
Edinburgh; if you are unable to travel there and research personally,
you might engage a professional genealogist to undertake work there.
There are companies in England which advertise Scottish research, but
they simply sub-contract the work to record agents in Scotland. It is
more satisfactory to employ a member of the Association of Scottish
Genealogists and Record Agents (see Chapter 10). The essential thing
to grasp when you employ a professional is that you must pay for that
person's time; but you can stipulate in advance how much you are
willing or able to spend.

It is possible for you to research Scottish basic records on microfilm if you are within reach of a branch library of the Church of
Jesus Christ of Latter Day Saints (the Mormons). Their Genealogical
Library in Salt Lake City can supply a list of more than 400 branch
libraries on request.   Members and non-members are charged the same
moderate fee.   They have on film all the **Old Parochial Registers of
Scotland**, old census returns, and parts of the post-1855 statutory
registers of births, deaths and marriages. All of their branches have
a copy of the **International Genealogical Index** (IGI), which is an
index to names in the computer of the Genealogy Department of the
Mormon Church.

When your researches have been completed you may wish to write a
family history. There are several methods: the short family history;
the anecdotal family history; the historical family history; the
scientific family history, on the lines of the tabulated articles in
Burk's Peerage; or the social and economic family narrative.   It is
not practical to choose which method to adopt until you have done considerable research, and then a reading of the introduction by Sir
James Balfour Paul (1846-1931), to Margaret Stuart's bibliography,
Scottish Family History (Edinburgh, 1930, reprinted Baltimore, 1978),
is recommended. You may be satisfied with a good typed copy, with
perhaps a few carbons, or--depending on your financial circumstances--
you may wish to publish or at least print for private circulation a
limited edition.   This should be carefully explored as there are
numerous methods of reproduction, even from typewriter script.

Grangemouth School-House,
12th August, 1850.

Sir,—

I request the favor of your company to attend the Funeral of my Husband, Malcolm McLaren, to the place of Interment, in Falkirk Church-yard, on Friday the 16th current, at Two o'clock p. m.

I am,

Sir,

Your very obedient Servant,

Jane McLaren.

Funeral intimation.

2. VITAL REGISTRATION

Statutory registration of births, marriages and deaths commenced in Scotland on 1st January, 1855, and was based more upon the French than the inferior English system which was instituted on 1st July, 1837. The genealogical content of the records is extremely good, but it should be remembered these were framed for legal and administrative purposes, and not with the needs of the pedigree hunter in mind. The volumes are preserved at New Register House, Edinburgh, in the care of the Registrar General for Scotland.

The birth certificates give the following particulars: 1) name and surname of child; 2) when and where born; 3) sex; 4) name, surname, rank or occupation of father, and name and surname of mother, with (except 1856-61) date of marriage; 5) signature and qualification of informant, and residence if out of the house or hospital in which the birth occurred; 6) when and where registered, and signature of registrar.

Marriage records contain the following information: 1) when and how married (for example, after proclamation); 2) names, in full, of the parties, with rank or occupation, and whether bachelor, spinster, widowed or divorced; 3) age of parties; 4) usual residence; 5) name, surname, and rank or occupation of the parents of both bride and groom, with a notation if deceased; 6) if a regular marriage, signature and designation of officiating clergyman or registrar (if an irregular marriage, date and declarator of Sheriff), and signatures of the witnesses; 7) when and where registered, and signature of registrar. Some slight changes appear in the certificates since the **Marriage (Scotland) Act**, effective from 1st January, 1978.

In the case of deaths the following particulars are recorded: 1) name and surname of the deceased, rank or occupation, and whether single, married or widowed; 2) when and where died; 3) sex; 4) age; 5) name, surname, rank or occupation of father, and name and maiden name of mother, with a notation if either was deceased; 6) cause of death, duration of illness, and name of physician by whom certified; 7) signature and qualification of informant, and residence if out of the house in which the death occurred; 8) when and where registered, and signature of registrar.

Occasionally, you may find a notation in the margin of a certificate, embracing the letters R.C.E., and a volume and page reference. This refers to the **Register of Corrected Entries**.

Alterations can mean that parents have changed the name of a child; that a divorce has taken place; or that cause of death has been established following preliminary examination.

If you start with the birth certificate of a child born in wedlock, you will have the date of the marriage of the parents. Then you can trace the certificate of marriage, which will provide the names of the four grandparents. There are indices for males and females, so the parties are cross-referenced. Next you can work out from the marriage certificate the ages of the parties, and trace their births if born after 1855. If born before then you can consult census returns to find their birthplaces, then try to find their baptisms in the **Old Parochial Registers**. After 1928 the maiden surnames of mothers are shown in the indices.

Since 1974 the maiden surnames of mothers are shown in the indices to the deaths. This has been facilitated by computer indexing, which caused the introduction of a loose-leaf system of recording in 1966. The indices of deaths for 1855-65 do not include ages; and unless you are sure of the registration district, the entries can only be found by a process of elimination. A pointer to future developments is the fact that from 1946 all the registers are available on microfiche. If your starting point is reasonably modern, you may find three or four generations of ancestors within the post-1855 period.

There has been an official census (except for the war periods) in Scotland every ten years since 1801, but the first four were merely statistical. Those records are also in the jurisdiction of the Registrar General. The first returns of value to the genealogist are contained in the **Census of Scotland**, 1841, which records the names of all persons in households, their occupations and ages (usually understated in the case of adults as the enumerators were instructed to write 20 for a person aged 20-25; 25 for a person aged 25-30, and so on). Unfortunately the returns do not give precise places of birth. It was only asked if people were born in the county of residence or not. Nor were relationships recorded, but the groups can often be compared with entries in the **Old Parochial Registers.**

The 1851 and later returns are of greater value as relationships are given, and places of birth, although if not born in Scotland only the country is stated. The returns up to 1891 are available for study (1841 and 1851 on microfilm only), and enable the researcher to assemble family groups, which can be checked against entries in the

CERTIFICATE OF PROCLAMATION OF BANNS.

Linlithgow   22nd February 1914

That Thomas Leslie   residing in the Parish of Low Carse, Glasgow   and Elizabeth Frances Connor residing in the Parish of Linlithgow   have been three times regularly proclaimed in the Parish Church here, in order to Marriage, and that no objections to the celebration of same have been offered, are certified by

William Dougal   Session Clerk.

By the Act of Parliament, 22 and 24 Victoria, chap. 85, sec. 15, the Certificate of Proclamation of Banns must be produced to the *Registrar of the Parish or District* within which *the Marriage* is to take place, when the necessary Marriage Schedule will be issued.

Certificate of Marriage.

The Manse, Feb 26. 1915

I hereby certify that the above-named Persons   Thomas Leslie
and Elizabeth Frances Connor

were this day Married by me.

Robert Oxspank B. Minister.

WORKSHEET FOR EXTRACTING SCOTTISH CENSUS SCHEDULES

No. of Parish or Reg. Dist.	775	Island of	—	Date of Census	11th April, 1871
Name of Parish or Reg. Dist.	Galashiels	Burgh of	—	Town or Village	13 Queen Street,
County	Selkirk	Schedule No.	94	Farm or Street	Galashiels.
Enumeration District	Galashiels	Book of Census	6	Page of Census	21
Condition of Record	good	Date of Search	10th October, 1977	Search No.	—

Name and Surname of Each Person	* Relationship	* Status	Age of M	Age of F	Rank, Profession or Occupation	Place of Birth
Donald Whyte	Head	Mar	55		Skinner's Labourer	Kilmun, Argyll
Mary do.	Wife	Mar		48	—	St. Boswells, Roxburghshire
John do.	Son	Unm	28		Railway Porter	Kilmun, Argyll
George Grant	Boarder	Unm	22		Rly. Signalman	Inverallan, Inverness
Euphemia Whyte	Daur	Unm		21	Woollen warp winder	Kilmun, Argyll
Violet do.	Daur	Unm		16	Power loom weaver woollen	Stow, Edinburgh
Isabella do.	Daur	—		14	yarn winder	Stow, Selkirkshire

Suggested that only one household appear on each sheet.
* Details not in 1841 returns.

Worksheets available from the
SCOTTISH GENEALOGY SOCIETY

statutory registers. For the larger towns, indices have been compiled, but only by streets. It is thus important to extract addresses
when copying out entries of births, marriages and deaths.

Having through the statutory registers and census returns got back
to 1855 or earlier, you should now consult the **Old Parochial Registers
of Scotland,** which are also in the custody of the Registrar General.
There are registers for some 900 parishes. These are gradually being
withdrawn and microfilm copies substituted for research purposes.
Although the history of parochial registers begins before the Scottish
Reformation of 1560, only about twenty parishes have records before
1600. Except for the Western Isles, where little was recorded before
1800, they are fairly regular from about 1740. These registers were
kept by the ministers or session-clerks of the Church of Scotland, and
are Presbyterian. Some clerks recorded events relating to people outside the Established Church, especially proclamations of marriages.

No uniform method of entering baptisms, proclamations or burials
was instituted, and the vagaries of human nature must be taken into
account. Moreover, church divisions, pulpit vacancies and other
events frequently caused blanks in the registers. Miscellaneous
matter sometimes appears, mainly session minutes relating to church
discipline. Where the names of sponsors or witnesses have been
entered, these should be extracted, as quite often a detailed break-
down will show relationships and shed light on naming customs. In the
case of proclamations, sometimes the name of the bride's father has
been recorded, but seldom the name of the bridegroom's father. The
fact of marriage is not always stated. Irregular marriages were often
confirmed after the parties had subjected themselves to church
discipline, and if no record appears among the proclamations, it is
worth consulting the Kirk-Session Records.

An "irregular" marriage was constituted by the parties consenting
without ceremony to take each other for husband and wife. In the main
the State, but not the Church, recognised three forms: the first was
a marriage by declaration; the second concerned a promise of physical
union; and the third by living together, becoming ultimately man and
wife **by habit and repute.** The latter is the only form of irregular
marriage surviving in Scotland today. Occasionally the older records
refer to a "clandestine" marriage. This was an irregular marriage
with some kind of religious ceremony, but which did not satisfy the
requirements of the Church.

The burial registers fared worst of all, except in the towns, where
the record need was greater. Frequently, only the name of the

deceased is entered, with the date of burial, but no age, cause of death or next of kin. Some of these records are still in local custody, and many have been lost. It was the custom of the kirk-sessions to hire out velvet cloths with which to cover the plain coffins, and occasionally the only record of death is found in these financial transactions.

In recent years an attempt has been made by the Mormons to index the **Old Parochial Registers of Scotland,** all of which they have microfilmed. At present microfiche indices are available for roughly the northern half of the country, and are compiled on a county basis.

There are a number of registers for churches other than those of the parishes, and it must be remembered that many were Presbyterian, relating to offshoots of the Established Church. A valuable collection of non-conformist records is held by the Scottish Record Office, in Edinburgh, and includes registers of Relief, Burgher, Free and United Free congregations, Methodist, Quaker and Episcopalian churches. Photographic reproductions of Roman Catholic records have been made.

The Registrar General has custody of a smaller collection of non-confromist registers. A noteworthy feature of this group is that it contains a number of Free Church baptismal records which bridge the gap so often found in the **Old Parochial Registers** between the Disruption of the Scottish Church in 1843, and the introduction of statutory registration in 1855. Fees are payable for access to all records in the care of the Registrar General.

Steill.

Testament testamentary of Thomas Steill in Crindildyke,
Cambusnethan, Lanarkshire, confirmed 17th August, 1635.
Commissariot Records of Glasgow. Reproduced by courtesy
of the Scottish Record Office.

Name and Designation.	Date of Recording.	Vol.	Fol.	County or Sheriffdom.
SPOTTISWOOD, MARGARET, spouse of William Mitchell in Black-syde.	14 Aug. 1618	1	217	Ayr
„ „ „ „	20 July 1624	3	106	„
STEILL, ADAM, son of Gilbert S. in Blookmylne .	6 Mar. 1621	2	127	„
„ „ „ „ „ .	6 „ 1621	2	129	„
„ ELIZABETH, in Gymishill . . .	22 June 1625	3	347	„
„ „ mother of Andrew Dick in Gymshill.	19 May 1624	3	75	„
„ ISOBEL ROBESONE, spouse of James, son of John S. in Comownecraig.	17 Nov. 1632	5	329	„
„ JAMES, son of John S. in Comownecraig .	17 „ 1632	5	329	„
„ JANET, spouse of William M'Kirrown in Fairley.	5 Feb. 1630	4	528	„
„ „ ANDREW, spouse of William, son of John S. in Jakishorne of Kil- maurs.	6 Mar. 1624	3	47	„
„ „ NEILSOUN (? WILSOUN), spouse of John, in Commownecraig.	13 Apr. 1629	4	381	„
„ „ WILSOUN (? NEILSOUN), spouse of John, in Comownecraig.	17 Nov. 1632	5	329	„
„ JOHN, in Commownecraig . . .	13 Apr. 1629	4	381	„
„ „ „ . . .	17 Nov. 1632	5	329	„
„ „ in Jacksthorn	30 Aug. 1617	1	13	„
„ „ in Jakishorne of Kilmaurs . .	6 Mar. 1624	3	47	„
„ „ in Jackisthorne, burgess of Kilmaurs	12 Aug. 1631	5	134	„
„ „ in Struthers	8 Sept. 1632	5	318	„
„ „ „	12 July 1634	6	231	„
„ MARGARET, spouse of John Gemmill, mason.	8 Aug. 1626	3	626	„
„ WILLIAM, in Jackisthorne . . .	12 „ 1631	5	134	„
„ „ „ . . .	1 Sept. 1631	5	151	„
„ „ son of John S. in Jakishorne of Kilmaurs.	6 Mar. 1624	3	47	„
STEVINSON (STEINSOUN, STEINSTOUN, STENESTOUNE).				
„ ADAM, in Mylntoun . . .	15 Feb. 1628	4	217	„
„ AGNES HOWIE, spouse of John, por- tioner of Quhytleys.	4 June 1619	1	347	„

3. THE SCOTTISH RECORD OFFICE

The S.R.O. in Edinburgh was established for the care of state papers and administrative records of pre-Union Scotland, registers of courts of law and commissary courts, but contains also material of more recent origin. The department is part of H.M. General Register House, which stands at the east end of Princes Street, adjacent to New Register House.

Many records which are valuable for their genealogical content are ecclesiastical in origin. This is true also of commissary court records, which are thought of primarily as registers of testaments and inventories. The earliest surviving records of this kind commenced before the Reformation: Edinburgh commissariot in 1514; Dunblane in 1539; Glasgow in 1547, and St. Andrew's in 1549. The upheaval of 1560 brought temporary confusion, but in 1564 a court was re-established at Edinburgh, and others followed.

These records are in the S.R.O., and there are two types: **Testament Testamentary**, where there is a will, with an executor nominated; and **Testament Dative**, where an inventory is given up by the person claiming right to "intromet" with the deceased person's estate, as nearest of kin or creditor--the person to be "confirmed" by the Commissary. The first words make the distinction clear, and in every case there is an inventory of the dead person's "goods, gear, debts and sums of money." The testament dative is disappointing if only genealogical data is sought, but these records are valuable to the social historian.

Indices for all the commissariots down to 1800 have been printed by the Scottish Record Society, and typescript indices exist at the S.R.O. for the period 1823-30, when the jurisdiction was transferred to the Sheriff Courts. Only moveables were willed in this form, and it is worth remembering that Edinburgh served as a general commissariot.

The records of testaments for modern times are among the Sheriff Court records, most of which have been transferred to the S.R.O. or its annex, West Register House, in Charlotte Square. Where the records have been deposited in Edinburgh, the repertory should be carefully consulted to ascertain what exists. There are no national or county indices before 1876, when a **Register of Confirmations** was commenced. However, there is a printed **Register of Defuncts**, mainly 1846-65 (Lothians from 1827), based on Sheriff Court Records.

The **Register of Deeds** has been described as "an inexhaustible store of information," about Scottish forefathers, and it flowed apparently as a matter of convenience from the Court of Session, instituted in 1532. It preserves bonds, protests, indentures, probatory writs, marriage contracts and other agreements.

Commencing in 1554, the first series extends to 627 volumes kept by various clerks to 1657. The second series dates from the Restoration of 1661, and is in three divisions representing the offices of the principal clerks, Dalrymple, Durie and Mackenzie, extending respectively to 313, 350 and 296 volumes, some of which are in two parts. The third series, dating from 1812, extends to more than 12,000 volumes, numbered consecutively. A **Calendar of Deeds** exists in manuscript for the period 1554-95, and there are indices for the years, 1661-95, 1750-53, and from 1770 onwards.

In medieval times, sasines, as well as deeds of various kinds were recorded by notaries in **Protocol Books,** many of which are in the S.R.O. A few have been printed by the Scottish Record Society and other bodies. A sasine may be described as the putting into possession of property, originally by handing over a symbol, for example for land a handful of earth, and later by registration of an instrument of sasine or of the conveyance itself.

Several attempts were made to regulate the recording of sasines, and in 1617 the Scottish Parliament enacted that general and particular registers be kept. The old **General Register of Sasines** runs from 1617-1868, and includes properties situated in more than one county or district. The **Particular Registers** cover separate territories, but occasionally two or more counties are included, such as Argyll and Bute.

In 1868 the Land Registers Act ordained that particular registers be closed, and henceforth there is a single **General Register,** still in use. An abridged printed register exists from 1781, and there are indices to parts of older registers. Where there is no index, it is helpful to consult the minute books, which are listed in a repertory at the S.R.O.

The sasines are now processed at Meadowbank House, Edinburgh, and are under the care of the Keeper of the Registers of Scotland, not to be confused with the Keeper of the Records of Scotland (at the S.R.O.). However, the older registers can be consulted in the Historical Search Room of the S.R.O. In addition to these records

there are separate registers for the Scottish burghs, which were
instituted in 1681, and ran to 1926, since which date the transactions
have been included in the **General Register**. Many burgh registers are
now in the S.R.O. A new **Land Registration (Scotland) Act**, was passed
in 1979, but so far its provisions have been extended only to a small
part of the country.

Another good source of information—especially where people have
died intestate—is the record of retours, which are so named from
being originally the return of a verdict of a jury in inquests proceeding upon brieves issued from the Chancery Office. This is largely
obsolete, but the Chancery has continued to deal with the service of
heirs, and the recording of services. It bears no resemblance to the
English Chancery. Writs are sealed in the Chancery with the Quarter
Seal (for example, gifts of *ultimis haeres*).

The earliest records of Chancery are wanting. Those covering the
period 1544-1699, have been printed in abstract in three folio volumes, titled **Inquisitionum ad Capellam Domini Regis Retornatarum . . .
Abreviatio**, edited by T. Thomson (Edinburgh, 1811-16). From 1700
there are **Decennial Indices**, which are abbreviated abstracts of great
value to the genealogist. These can be consulted at the S.R.O. and
some of the larger libraries. The originals often survive, and there
is a register—generally in Latin—which can be consulted for fuller
details.

The **Hearth Money Accounts** of 1690-93, preserved at the S.R.O. give
the names of heads of households which had hearths. While these give
less information than **Poll-Tax Records**, they cover a larger part of
the country, and are useful for places for which no poll-tax records
exist. In 1693 the Scottish Parliament imposed, over and above an
existing land tax, a poll-tax to pay debts due to the army and navy.
It was levied in 1694 and again in 1695, but the amount of detail in
the rolls varies.

By an agreement of 1960 between the Church of Scotland and the
Keeper of the Records of Scotland, a historic collection of records
preserved in the General Assembly Library were transferred to the
S.R.O. on long loan. The transmission contains older records of the
General Assembly, records of synods and presbyteries, and kirk-session
records. Included are records of other Presbyterian churches which
have united with the Church of Scotland. A list of these records was
printed by the Scottish Record Society in 1967.

A vast collection of manuscripts has been gifted or deposited on long loan to the S.R.O. by individuals and companies. These vary in antiquity and importance. Entries for the **Gifts and Deposits** series are contained in a **Summary Catalogue.** Details of estate papers for a cross-section can be found in **List of Gifts and Deposits** (Edinburgh, 1971 and 1976). Material for countries such as U.S.A., Canada, Australia, New Zealand, West Indies and Africa, has been grouped. **A List of American Documents** was published in 1976. Historical material in private hands has been extensively catalogued by the National Register of Archives, a department of the S.R.O. There is also an extensive collection of maps and estate plans.

It is worthwhile, when researching families who have owned land in the earlier times, to consult the unpublished **Calendar of Register House Charters** (15 volumes and indices), and the **Register of the Great Seal of Scotland,** of which abstracts have been printed, 1306-1668. There are typescript indices at the S.R.O. covering later registers. Early charters in **Regesta Regum Scotorum,** edited by Professor G.W.S. Barrow and others, shed light on the development of surnames. The **Register of Entails,** instituted in 1685, is also a mine of information regarding landed families.

Scotland does not have county record offices like England, but in recent years many regional and district archives have been created or expanded. Much of the material being preserved is historical rather than genealogical, but family and estate papers can be helpful. If you had ancestors who lived in an old Scottish burgh, you should establish if records relating to merchant guilds or craft incorporations exist. A few such bodies have published histories; Glasgow is especially fortunate in this respect as these organizations exist there more strongly than elsewhere, although their exclusive privileges were abolished in 1846. The Scottish Records Association has printed numerous summaries of archival holdings (**Datasheet** No. 6), of regions, districts and universities. These show that much has survived of records of merchants and trades fraternities.

4. SERVICE RECORDS

Previous to the 17th Century Scotland never had a standing army, and simply relied on feudal military service when the need arose. At such times Scots who had soldiered under Continental and Scandinavian flags figured prominently as officers. As there was no military bureaucracy there are no specifically army records. The main sources for the pre-Cromwellian era are the records of Parliament and the registers of the Privy Council, Treasury and Exchequer.

Numerous muster rolls have been preserved among the Treasury records at the S.R.O., and the **Register of the Privy Council**, printed 1545-1691, contains fascinating references to military matters, as well as a wealth of genealogical material. Printed sources include C.S. Terry's **Life and Campaigns of Alexander Leslie** (London, 1899), and his **Papers Relating to the Army of the Solemn League & Covenant** (Edinburgh: Scottish Record Society, 1917); and C. Dalton's **The Scots Army**, 1661-88 (London, 1909). A scarce pamphlet listing officers taken prisoner by Cromwell's army at Dunbar in 1651, is preserved among the **Thomason Tracts**, at the Public Record Office, London. A microfilm of the collection is now available at the National Library of Scotland, George IV. Bridge, Edinburgh.

After the Union of the Parliaments of Scotland and England in 1707, the records of the Scottish regiments become a part of the British Army records held at the P.R.O., and these include fencible regiments, militia and volunteers. Dalton's **English Army Lists**, 1616-1714 (London, 1892-1904), 6 volumes, is a useful work. Several volumes relating to the Jacobite Army, including **Prisoners of the '45**, have been printed by the Scottish History Society.

The first attempt to compile regular lists of army officers was made in 1733 by Capt. T. Desibray, a Dublin army agent, or his clerks, but these rolls only dealt with regiments on the Irish establishment. It was not until 1754 that the **Annual Army List** appeared. A monthly list was produced from 1798-1808. Quarterly lists commenced in 1880. Bibliographical details of these, and fencible, militia and yoemanry lists are contained in an article by A.S. White in Vol. 25 of the **Journal of Army Historical Research** (pp. 118-127), supplemented in vol. 45 (pp. 32-34) by data relating to lists from 1939-60. Of unofficial lists the most important are those by Lt. H.G. Hart, notably a quarterly publication which appeared from 1838-1914, and an annual list, 1840-1915. Printed army lists are held by the Copyright

Libraries, and by some military institutions, as well as by the
Scottish United Services Museum, at Edinburgh Castle.

Researchers often have difficulty in identifying Scottish regiments, because of amalgamations, or by the complexities of the num-
bering system. Space does not permit accounts of famous regiments of
the past, such as the 77th Regiment (Montgomery's Highlanders),
1757-1763, engaged in America during the Seven Years War, and the
Royal Highland Emigrant (84th) Regiment, raised in America for service
during the Revolution, but the charts on Plate VIII, showing the
Scottish Division of the British Army, will be of assistance to family
historians.

Apart from old disbanded regiments, service battalions, terri-
torials, yoemanry and others, there are two other regiments of the
British Army forever associated with Scotland. These are The Scots
Guards, who can trace their ancestry to a regiment raised by the
Marquis of Argyle in 1642, and the Royal Scots Greys, whose history
dates back to 1678-81, when six troops of dragoons were raised to cope
with the Covenanting troubles. They became the only regiment of
Scottish cavalry and the oldest regiment of dragoons in the British
Army. In 1971 they were merged with the 3rd Carabineers to form the
Royal Scots Dragoons.

It has been remarked that Scotland never had a navy in the national
sense of the word, but as with the military, much curious information
will be found among the records of Parliament, the Privy Council and
Exchequer. The early history is brought together in the introduction
to James Grant's book, **The Old Scots Navy**, 1689-1710 (London: Navy
Records Society, 1914). It is also worth remembering that Scotland
had its own High Court of Admiralty until 1830.

Scots who served in the English Navy or in the British Navy may be
sought among the voluminous Admiralty records at the P.R.O. in London.
For ratings the **Muster Rolls** will be found helpful. Many officers are
noticed in J. Marshall's **Royal Navy Biography**, 12 vols. (London,
1823-30), and in W.R. O'Byrne's **Naval Biographical Dictionary** (London,
1849).

Lloyd's **Marine Collection** of records and publications is now in the
Guildhall Library, Aldermanbury, London, and is available for research
on weekdays. Included are the **Mercantile Navy List**, 1857-1970;
Captain's Registers, 1868-1947, containing information about all

HIGHLAND REGIMENTS

Origins	1881 groupings	Intermediate	Modern
1739 43rd Regiment, formed from six independ-ent companies. Renumbered 42nd. 1758 2nd Battalion formed and became 73rd Regiment.	The 42nd Royal Highland Regiment of Foot, amalgamated with The 73rd (Perthshire Regiment of Foot).	1st and 2nd Battalions, The Black Watch (Royal Highland-ers).	The Black Watch (Royal Highland Regiment).
1757 63rd Regiment or Fraser's Highlanders, renumbered in 1758 as the 78th Highlanders. 1778 78th Highlanders or Seaforth Regiment, re-numbered 72nd, 1786. 1793 Cameron Volunteers or 79th Regiment.	The 78th Highland Regiment of Foot (Ross-shire Buffs), amalgamated with The 72nd (Duke of Albany's Own Highlanders). The 79th (Queen's Own Cameron Highlanders Regiment). 2 Battalions.	1st and 2nd Battalions, The Seaforth Highlanders, amalgamated in 1960 with The Queen's Own Cameron Highlanders	The Queen's Own Highlanders.
1787 75th (Highland) Regiment of Foot. 1794 100th Regiment of Foot, renumbered 92nd	The 75th (Stirling-shire) Regiment of Foot. amalgamated with 92nd (Gordon Highlanders) Regiment of Foot.	1st and 2nd Battalions The Gordon Highlanders	The Gordon Highlanders
1794 98th Argyllshire Regiment, renumbered 91st. 1800 93rd Highlanders, formed mainly from the Sutherland Fencible Regiment.	91st (Princess Louise's) Argyllshire Highlanders, amalgamated with 93rd Sutherland Highlanders.	1st and 2nd Battalions Argyll & Sutherland Highland-ers.	The Argyll & Sutherland Highlanders (1st Battalion disbanded in 1970, but re-raised, 1972)

LOWLAND REGIMENTS

	Origins	1881 groupings	Intermediate	Modern
1633	Hepburn's Regiment, became Ist Regiment of Foot.	The Royal Scots (Lothian Regiment), 2 Battalions.	The Royal Scots (The Royal Regiment)	The Royal Scots (The Royal Regiment).
1678	Earl of Mar's Regiment, or The Scots Fusiliers Regiment of Foot.	21st (Royal North British Fusiliers) Regiment of Foot.	The Royal Scots Fusiliers amalgamated in 1959 with	Royal Highland Fusiliers (Princess Margaret's Own Glasgow and Ayrshire Regiment).
1777	Lord MacLeod's Highlanders, numbered 73rd Regiment of Foot.	71st (Glasgow Highland Light Infantry Regiment).	71st Highland Light Infantry	
1689	Earl of Leven's, or Edinburgh Regiment of Foot, numbered 73rd.	The 25th (King's Own Borderers) Regiment of Foot. 2 Battalions.	The King's Own Borderers	The King's Own Scottish Borderers.
1689	The Cameronians.	The 26th Regiment of Foot, amalgamated with	Ist and 2nd Battalions, The Cameronians (Scottish Rifles), disbanded 1968	The Cameronians. Name and uniform continued by Cameronian Companies of the Territorial and Volunteer Reserve, Kelvinside Cadets, and Lanarkshire Battalion of the Army Cadet Force.
1794	90th (Perthshire Volunteers) Regiment.	The 90th (Perthshire Volunteers) (Light Infantry).		

THE ROYAL SCOTS GREYS
[2nd Dragoons]

SCOTS GUARDS

holders of Master's certificates; Lloyd's **Confidential Index,**
1886-1920, which lists owners and their fleets; and the **Weekly
Shipping Index,** 1880-1917, which includes casualty reports. Petitions
to Trinity House from Scottish seamen or their dependents for
assistance during the years 1780-1854, are now in the Library of the
Society of Genealogists, 14 Charterhouse Buildings, London, EC1M 7BA.

Post 1855 sources under the supervision of the Registrar General
for Scotland include marine, air and army registers. The certified
returns for shipping and seamen are in respect of births and deaths on
British vessels at sea, if the child's father or the deceased person
was a Scot. An air register has a record of births and deaths in
aircraft registered in the United Kingdom, where it appears the
child's father or the deceased person was usually resident in
Scotland. The returns to the Registrar General include births,
marriages and deaths of Scottish persons at military stations abroad
during the period 1883-1959; the Service Department's registers since
1st April, 1959, which have recorded births, marriages and deaths outside the U.K. relating to persons who were serving or employed by H.M.
Forces; and certified copies of entries relating to marriage solem-
nised outside the U.K. by army chaplains since 1892, where one of the
parties is described as Scottish, and at least one of them was serving
with the Forces. For births of children of members of the Forces
serving abroad, the **Consular and Foreign Returns** held by the Registrar
General should also be checked. From 1975 events relating to Scots
people overseas are included in the annual indices to the statutory
registers, and a microfiche index covering the years 1855-1974 is
available.

There are **War Registers** accessible to researchers at New Register
House, and these fall into three divisions. The first covers the
deaths of Scottish soldiers during the South African War (1899-1902);
the second relating to World War I (1914-19), records the deaths of
Scottish persons serving as Warrant Officers, Non-Commissioned
Officers or men of the Army or of the Royal Navy; while the third con-
sists of incomplete records of deaths in World War II (1939-45), of
Scottish members of the Forces.

Most of the War Office Records are in the Public Record Office in
London. These include muster rolls, description books, pensioned
soldiers documents, Chelsea Hospital **Admission Books,** and records of
courts martial. The best guide to official records is **In Search of
Army Ancestry,** by Gerald Hamilton Edwards (London & Chichester, 1977).

For units of the British army, researchers should also consult **A Bibliography of Regimental Histories**, by A.S. White (London, 1965).

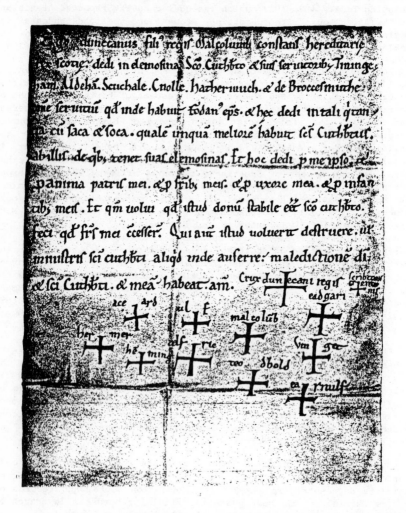

5. ORIGINS OF SURNAMES

William Camden, the first serious student of British surnames, wrote: "Every person had in the beginning only one proper name," and if we look at early record sources for Scotland, we find that personal names predominate. In the charter of King Duncan to the monks St. Cuthbert, granted in 1094, no surnames appear. The monarch and the witnesses made their rude crosses, over which the scribe Grento added their names: Aceard, Hermer, Hemming, Ulf, Aelfric, Malcolumb, Teobold, Duncan the King, Eadgar, Vinget and Earnulf.

Sur or additional names (not sire names) are of comparatively late origin, and often appear in changed or corrupt form. They emerged slowly, and we can detect the evolution in early charters. That granted during the reign of David I (1124-53) by Waldeve, son of Cospatrick, to Helias, son of Huchtred, of the lands of Dundas, has among the witnesses, Waldeve, son of Baldwin, William of Copeland and Adam the Steward. Baldwin may have become a surname through the dropping of "son of," but this is a written form and such a conclusion would be dubious. However, Copeland--a place-name--emerged as a sur-name, and Steward (or Stewart) did likewise.

The process grew with an increase in population and mobility in the 13th century. In small communities, personal names were sufficient, and patronymics were all that custom required. Throughout many parts of the world surnames are still a rarity. Until the early 19th century, patronymics alone served the needs of many closely knit communities in the Highlands and Islands of Scotland.

Surnames may be divided into five groups, with some overlapping. There are those derived from the personal name of the father, more correctly termed surnames of relationship. Patronymics come into this class, although these produced surnames under varying circumstances. Then come names stemming from places, and these form a large group. Next are hundreds of trade or office names, usually referred to as occupational surnames. Into a fourth class, which we choose to call divergent names, come surnames flowing from a number of sources. Lastly there are surnames derived from nicknames, personal traits and characteristics.

Easily recognised as emerging from personal names--themselves deriving from a variety of sources--are surnames such as Allan, Henry, Thomas, and of course Adam. Before the Christian era personal names could claim numerical superiority; but since then, local, trade and divergent names have left these in the minority. Thousands might receive their name from a locality, but not even two could be called Jacob or Moses, except through a second-hand use by adoption or popular application.

Patronymics commonly indicate whose son a man is, and they were borne in ancient times as we can see from the *ben* and *bar* of the Semitic languages. In the Homeric lists of heroes they can be identified by the suffixes *ades* and *ides*. The Romans too, had their patronymic forms.

With the fall of the Roman Empire, the system of nomenclature declined. In Latin documents men came to be linked simply with the personal name of the father, for example Hugo filius Walterus, meaning Hugh, son of Walter. The Teutonic nations added *sen* or *son* to the personal name, while the Saxon style was the addition of *ing*, as in Atheling (Athel's son). In Welsh, a form of the Celtic *mac* emerged, which the Cambrians made *mab*, or *map*, shortened to *ap*. The Irish, being Celts, also used *mac*, son of, as a prefix, but often found greater charm in *ua*, originally a grandson, but by an extension of meaning any descendant. It is often written *hua*, by Latin and English writers, and still oftener *O*, which is a common prefix in Irish surnames.

In Scotland the Gaels used the prefix *mac* to denote son of, but frequently there was no real surname until a late period, and often it was a remote ancestor of note whose personal name became the fixed surname. The MacDonald chiefs derived their name from the mighty Somerled, Lord of the Isles.

Love of description and genealogy gave rise to patronymics such as Dhomnuill mac Chalum 'ic Alastair 'ic Iain Bhain (Donald, son of Malcolm, son of Alexander, son of Fair John). Examples of stabilised Gaelic surnames are: MacAlpine (son of Alpine); MacDermid (son of Dermid); MacEachin (son of Hector); MacLaren (son of Laurin or Lawrence); and MacPhail (son of Paul). Many derive from trades and offices: Maceachern (son of the horse lord); Macgowan (son of the smith); Maclellan (son of the devotee of St. Fillan); Macintosh (son of the leader); and Macintyre (son of the carpenter).

In ordinary English usage the form *son* is often appended to the Christian name, such as Thomson and Johnson, but some require a little thought: names like Dawson, an abbreviation of Davidson, and Watson, an shortening of Walterson.

Islandic naming pattern:

ARNAR   ASGEIR
| |

GUNNAR   SIGURLIN
Arnarson   *Asgeirsdotter*

ARNAR
Gunnarson

Many countries still do not have surnames, and Iceland
is a good example. The telephone books show given names.

Numerous surnames have their origin in place-names: counties, provinces, districts, sheriffdoms, towns, villages, hamlets, lordships, baronies, estates, farms and crofts. A good number have hardly changed, and point unmistakeably to the places which inspired them. Examples are Crawford, Cunningham, Dunbar, Home, Norton, Angus, Buchan, Glasgow and Galloway. Some are not easily recognised as they appear in archaic or distorted form.

When we consider national names, we generally find that a man had to move before these became applicable. A man from south of the border would be Englis, and modern forms are English and Englander. There are more Scot(t)s in England than in Scotland. The surname Dutch, found in the Firth of Tay area, is said to derive from a survivor of a Dutch man-of-war shipwrecked near Tayport during the reign of Queen Anne. Wallace is a historic surname in Scotland, and originates in the old kingdom of Strathclyde.

The non-resident principle can often be noted by record scholars. Surnames like Lothian and Berwick crop up in Fife from an early period. People in the Orkney Islands called Mainland are doubtless descended from a person or persons from the north of Scotland, probably Caithness.

Job-description is a much-used--and in trade union matters occasionally abused--term today; but for many centuries the surnames of numerous officials and tradesmen proclaimed their calling. Frequently son succeeded father in a particular trade because the tools were inherited. Curiously, the ancients were reluctant to adopt trade names. This was not through want of appreciating the dignity of labour, but because they were reluctant to change a name which recalled brave deed or hallowed relationship. Moreover, they may have been influenced by the fact that occupational surnames are sometimes indefinite. One man in a community might be called Jacob, while dozens might be named Smith as the metal craft embraced a number of trades.

Many occupational names are easily understood: Gardener, Taylor, Cook, Baker or Baxter, Cooper, Glover, Dyer, Skinner, Wright and Weaver. Likewise numerous official names are recognisable: Usher, Marshall, Carver, Steward, Porter and Page, all derive from the multiplicity of functions in the great houses and establishments of the Middle Ages. Some others require a little thought. Barker is from the obsolete name for the man who prepared the bark of trees for the Tanner. Condiner or Cordwainer comes from the man who made shoes of goatskin which was supposed to come from Cordova in Andalusia. With other shoemakers (Soutar is from this source) and workers in leather they formed fraternities in the old Scottish burghs. Potinger comes from *potage*, and indicates a maker of soups. Stoddart comes from stot-herd, *stot* being a general term for a young bull or bullock.

Surnames derived from nicknames form an interesting group, but many have disappeared because of their coarseness. Some can be taken literally, but others have a contrary meaning, in the way that "Tiny" is often used to describe a six-footer. Broadhead, Foot, Cudlipp and Longman all describe physical attributes or peculiarities, while Careless, Loveless, Sharp and Goodenough particularise mental and moral character.

Flett is probably Old Norse, meaning an eager fellow, or a flayer or robber. Scollay, found in the Orkney Islands, is apparently from the same source, *skalli* meaning bald-head. A few names which ended in head have been reduced to leave the suffix *ett*, as in Blackett, Brockett, Duckett and Strickett (*stirk-head*). Names of animals can be nicknames, but must be treated with caution. Lamb may denote weakness, and Bull great strength, but might come from a herd or keeper of these animals and be occupational surnames.

A significant number of divergent surnames come from plants, flowers, animals and birds, examples being Mustard, Primrose, Goodlamb and Swan. Many are derived from mediaeval pageantry and religious festivals, as illustrated in Prophet, Priest, King, Marquis, Duke, Bishop and Abbot. A few come from costumes or adjuncts of these, cases being Staff, Clubb, Bracegirdle and Broadbelt. Then there are war names like Brand (sword) and Randal (shield). A large number are mythological or biblical.

FOUR ANCIENT KINGDOMS.

6. CLANS AND FAMILIES

To understand the structure of clans and families it is worth remembering that the parts of the country we now recognise as Celtic formed the kingdom of Dalriada and part of Pictavia. Dalriada consisted of Argyll and the adjacent islands, and was colonised by Scots from Ireland about A.D. 500. The Pictish kingdom, stretching from the Firth of Forth, north and east of Drumalban--the great central ridge of the Highlands--was peopled by an earlier migration. The southern part of Scotland comprised mainly two other kingdoms: Strathclyde in the west, inhabited by Britons (Cymri or Welsh), perhaps remote relatives of the Picts, who were subject to the influences of the other kingdom, Bernicia, which stretched from the Forth to the Humber, and was peopled by Angles.

Kenneth MacAlpin, King of Scots, extended his sway over Pictavia or Calendonia in 844; and by the time of Malcolm Canmore, who married the Saxon Princess Margaret about 1068, the country was becoming subject to one monarch. The sons of Malcolm and Margaret developed the Norman system of government in Scotland. They were quick to grasp the practical advantages of a highly organised society, and to strengthen their administration, brought Norman and Anglo-Norman families to Scotland.

In time, as sheriffdoms and royal burghs were created in the Lowlands lands and up the east coast, where trade with Scandinavia and Europe developed, the Gaels were either absorbed into the Anglo-Saxon society, or gradually retreated into the mountains. The so-called "Highland Line" does not run from east to west, but diagonally across the country, roughly from Renfrew to Buchan Ness. Some historians extend the line some 10-20 miles inland from Peterhead all the way to Dunnet Head, on the Pentland Firth, but this is untenable.

Of course the imaginary line did not actually separate Gael from Lowlander, and overlapping has caused some problems for family historians. It has been fashionable since the time of Sir Walter Scott (1771-1832), to dress all families up as clans. An honest historian of the Grahams says it is "a moot point whether they can be considered a clan in the accepted sense of the word." The Grahams were certainly a Lowland family, but the Menteith line owned lands peopled by Gaels. This was also true of the Drummonds (titular Dukes of Perth), another Lowland family. At the northern extremity of the line the Gordons have also posed questions. One writer describes their territory as "something of a borderland, since the soil and climate are not strictly Highland." If we consult **Historical Geography of the Clans**, the concept of a "Highland Line" becomes more meaningful, with the folding map showing clans appearing in rolls of 1587 and 1594. The line is even further west than Buchan Ness, but shows part of Gordon territory in the Highlands. There is no suggestion of a line or coastal band extending to the Pentland Firth.

It was not the weather or the quality of the soil that made a clan. The very word **clann** (children, descendants) is ancient Gaelic, brought from Ireland by the Scots, and the clan itself was a Celtic organisation acknowledging one chief upon whom the people depended for justice and protection. The people--if not always the chiefly line--were distinctly Celtic in language, dress, social and agricultural customs, music, songs and poetry.

Original clan lands were within recognisable geographic limits: sometimes a small range of hills, a few glens or a cluster of islands. Some writers claim that without feudalism we would not have had a clan system. In fact, long after the embryo stage, many chiefs had no written title. Landowners with large scattered territories could not live as tribal patriarchs, and this was a strong reason for holding their lands by charter. For similar motives, many were given baronial powers. The Breadalbane Campbells, whose majority of tenants were not Campbells, and did not adopt that surname, are a good example. The Feudo-Celtic aspect however, did assist landowners to perpetuate the functions of tribal leaders.

We know so little of the clan organisation in ancient times that some writers have dated its commencement from the close of the 13th century. Perhaps they are attempting to justify the theory that the system could not have evolved without feudalism. If we look at the royal Irish clans and the succession through the law of tanistry to chiefships in Scotland, we can trace their development, although at a later period they differed from the Irish in having a class of administrators between them and the monarch. The Lordship of the Isles was influential, and in the north hereditary *maormors* arose, with jurisdiction over provinces such as Angus, Atholl, Mar and Moray. They may have been the successors of Pictish provincial royal chiefs, and they were the forerunners of the landed nobility.

The old Gaelic terminology continued in Dalriada and spread over the Highlands. *Cinel* (kinel) means tribe or kindred, and *siol* (shiel) means seed or progeny. The descendants of Fergus Mor, founder of the dynasty, through two grandsons, were called the *Cinel Comgall* and the

Drop Line Chart

WILLIAM DOV[...]
Monikie, Angu[...]

| SUSAN b. 1765 | MARION b. 1767 | BARBARA b. 1769 | GEORGE 1770–1852 | = AGNES HOGG | A[...] b. [...] |

| WILLIAM d. inf. | ALEXANDER b. 1802, d. inf. | ALEXANDER b. 1803 mill manager at Glamis | = ANN, dau. of JAMES GRIEVE St. Vigeans. | SAMUEL 1804–81 Engineer in New Zealand | = |

| GEORGE 1826–1903 m. 1852 farmer | = JEAN, dau. of JOHN JOHNSTON master builder, & JANET ALEXANDER | SAMUEL b. 1835 went to Co. Fermanagh, Ireland | = GEORGINA DEMPSTER | ALEXANDER GRIEVE b. 1837 | MA[...] AN[...] b. 18[...] |

ALEXANDER
GRIEVE
1852–67

JANET JOHNSTON
b. 1855
Glamis

ANN PETRIE

WILLIAM
b. 1774

ANDREW
b. 1778

JE, dau. of
LIAM BOURNE
uckland, N.Z.

BARBARA
b. 1807

DAVID
1808-38

= JEAN
TOD

GEORGE
b. 1812
millwright

= BETSY LOW
Dundee.

WILLIAM
BOURNE
d. inf.

JOHN
THOMAS
b. 1838,
Australia.

JANE
AMELIA
b. 1840

GEORGE
ALEXANDER
b. 1842
went to
So. Africa

MARY
AGNES
b. 1844

HARRIET
CURTIS
b. 1847

ELIZABETH
BOURNE
b. 1849

CATHERINE
HUTTON
1851-1936

VICTORIA
ANN
1854-1936

GRIEVE
1857
amis

= JOHN ELLSON

HELEN ROBERTSON
1860-87

Cinel Gabhran. The latter was the royal line from which sprang Kenneth MacAlpin, who united the Scots and Picts. It is significant that the early style was not King of Scotland, but in keeping with the patriarchal tradition--King of Scots.

Many clan chiefs had bardic legends of descent from the early kings. The MacKinnons, Macnabs, MacAulays, MacQuarries, Grants and MacGregors, were all thought to be of the *Siol Alpin*, and thus collateral lines of the monarchy. The MacGregors claimed seniority, and their motto is *S'reoghail mo dhream* ("my race is royal"). Modern scholarship points to descent from the old dynastic tribe of Ross.

It is a fallacy to imagine that clans consisted of people of the same surname, with a common ancestor, along with surnames brought in through marriage. Clans were made up of the chiefly line and its cadets, who were the principal gentry and tacksmen (lessees, who sublet their lands). Where the chiefs were non-Celtic, like the Frasers, Chisholms and Gordons, there may also have been indigenous people or natives, who may or may not have adopted their surnames. In addition there were hereditary officers and craftsmen who were not always of the same race. Sometimes there were "broken men" from other clans.

These elements have given rise to what are called sept-names. Lists of septs in books about clans and tartans should be treated with caution. Smith for example is given as a sept of Clan Chattan, but a little thought will show there must have been a Smith ('Gobha' = *gown*) in every clan, although in some cases "Gobha" remained an epithet. Houston is usually shown as a sept of Clan Donald, but the reference is only to *Clan Huistean*: The MacDonalds of Sleat. The Houstons are a Renfrewshire family.

The system of clanship in the Highlands was in principle different from the feudal system as observed in the rest of the country. In the one case people in a hunting and pastoral state of society followed their chief as the patriarch of their race, while in the other the people, possessing rude notions of agriculture, obeyed their leader as feudal proprietor of the lands to which they were attached. Of course Lowland barons placed cadets on lands within their sphere of influence, and many were recognised as chiefs of the surname. There was scant appearance of the patriarchal spirit, except along the English border, where the geographic features bear some resemblance to the Highlands.

The social system of the Highlands has been much admired, and clan societies attempt to recapture the traditions of tribality and inheritance. There is no good reason however, why people of Lowland descent should lament not belonging to a clan. On the contrary they should be proud of the contributions made to life and culture by Lowlanders.

Religious freedom and educational advances resulting from the Reformation of the Scottish Church in 1560, have had far-reaching effects. Some of the credit must go to the brave Covenanters, who preserved the democratic processes of Presbyterianism. Within the essentially English framework of Britain's former colonies, Lowland Scottish influences were of some importance in shaping their destinies. The Scottish universities--all in the Lowlands--made considerable impact on the early colleges of America.

In the countryside the people had their own traditions and folklore, enshrined in the works of Henryson, Dunbar, Ferguson, Hogg, Scott and Burns. The Lowland lairds pioneered new methods of husbandry: enclosing the land with belts of trees, dykes and hedges, liming the soil and improving the drainage. Among them were John Clerk of Penicuik, John Cockburn of Ormiston and Robert Maxwell of Arkland. Other landowners organised themselves to promote learning. The Highlander often had to go abroad to realise his potential; but Lowlanders made progress in every branch of knowledge, especially in the burghs, where the canny merchants and craftsmen must often have thought of the Highlander as barbarians.

7. HERALDRY AND TARTANS

In Scotland, heraldry is exceptionally well governed, because the Law of Arms and the Court of the Lord Lyon have survived the Union of 1707 intact, with a statutory **Register of all Arms and Bearings** (called **Lyon Register**), dating from 1672. Some older heraldic manuscripts, while not "official," are authentic; in fact the **Armorial Register of Sir David Lindsay**, c. 1540, the original of which is in the National Library of Scotland, cannot be questioned.

The Lord Lyon King of Arms--Scotland's principal heraldic and genealogical executive--is an Officer of State, who, with his procurator fiscal, heralds and pursuivants, still exercises his ancient powers. He is responsible for the conduct and preparation of Royal, State and Public ceremonial. In his armorial jurisdiction he stands in place of the Sovereign, and all grants of Arms flow through him to subjects of the Crown.

In Scotland, the importance of the Lord Lyon is due in part to his incorporating the pre-heraldic office of High Sennachie to the Royal Family. As preserver of the Royal lineage his oration at Coronations was essential. The venerable Highland bard who functioned at the Coronation of Alexander III. in 1249, was the predecessor of the Lord Lyon. Heraldic duties were in due course blended with the retaining of genealogies.

The name "Lyon" is derived from the rampant lion, which is still the emblem of the Royal line of Scotland. (Unicorns appear to have been introduced as supporters of the Royal Arms by James II, whose reign commenced in 1437). The prefix "Lord" has been in use since the 16th century, and no other European herald was vested with such high dignity. As the Controller of Her Majesty's Messengers at Arms, the Lord Lyon is the head of the executive department of the law of the realm, and on all matters relating to honours, titles and ceremonial, he is the advisor to the Secretary of State for Scotland.

The term "Coat-of-Arms" is derived from the picturesque tabards worn by knights over their armour, either in battle or during tournaments or joustings which gave proof of skills in martial arts. Conventional designs were in use prior to the 11th century, but it was during the 12th century that these became traditional and hereditary. Among the oldest Scottish armorial bearings are those displayed on the seals of Allan, High Steward of Scotland, c. 1177, and Patrick, Earl of Dunbar, c. 1182.

Despite increased fees for grants and matriculations, as well as for the illumination of scrolls, heraldry is popular. The legal effect is to confer on "virtuous and well-deserving persons," formal recognition by the Crown, and to grant the devised Coat-of-Arms for life, fully protected against usurpation. The heir may succeed to the undifferenced Arms, and younger sons can matriculate with the appropriate mark of difference. The system does not exclude women, and it has long been the custom (H.M. the Queen excepted) that the insignia appear on a lozenge (diamond shape), rather than on the warlike and masculine shield.

The descendants of armigerous families may matriculate in **Lyon Register**, depending on the "destination" of the original grant, and it is always worth investigating the possibility of qualifying. New grants are not normally made to foreigners, but it is possible to petition for armorial bearings for an ancestor born in Scotland, and to matriculate as a descendant.

Corporate bodies in Scotland, such as regional and district councils, companies, clubs or any other formally established group of people may apply for Arms. The Scottish Genealogy Society was granted armorial bearings in 1978, and can use these in the same way as a private person to signify its identity and to adorn its products or publications. Moreover, members in good standing may wear the Society's armorial badge.

When sitting in full court the Lord Lyon wears a robe of crimson velvet, and for other ceremonials he and his officers dress in tabards. However, due to their courtesy, the ordinary business of petitioning for Arms can be conducted "without wig or gown." The Lyon Office--which contains a valuable library--is situated in a wing of New Register House, Edinburgh.

Tartans do not have the precise distinctions and recognisability of armorial bearings, and it would be imprudent to claim that multi-coloured or striped costume is peculiar to Scotland. The word "tiretaine" was originally given by the French to a certain type of fabric, regardless of colour. The Gaels used the term *breacan* for speckled or parti-coloured material.

Coloured apparel dates back to biblical times, but cannot be identified with what we call tartan. However, a costume found in a Jutland grave in 1879, and considered to be older than the Turin

CREST-BADGE:

MacLeod

The Crest of the Chief is <u>worn</u> by all members of the Clan and of approved Septs and followers of the Clan, within a strap and buckle surround bearing the Chief's motto. This is for <u>personal wear only</u>, to indicate that the wearer is a member of the Clan whose Chief's crest-badge is being worn. The badge or crest is <u>not</u> depicted on personal or business stationery, signet rings or plate, because such use would legally import that the tea-pot, etc., was the Chief's property!

Reproduced by courtesy of the Lyon Office.

**Armorial Bearings of
the Scottish Genealogy
Society**

BLAZON: Azure, on a saltire Argent between in chief a lion's head erazed
Or, langued Gules, in base an oak tree fructed Or, and in each
flank a septfoil Argent, a patriarchal cross Gules, and in an
escrol below the same this motto: "FOR FAMILY AND NATION."
(*Lyon Register*, LIX, 108).

DRAWING: Institute of Heraldic & Genealogical Studies, Canterbury,
Kent.

shroud, bears a startling resemblance to tartan. It is now in the
Danish National Museum, at Copenhagen.

The earliest written reference to Highland dress
may well be the ordinances of the diocese of
Aberdeen, 1256, directing the clergy to avoid
striped clothing: red and green. Highland costume, in most early accounts, seems distinguished
by the shoulder covering. The belted plaid of
later times was a single, all-purpose garment, from
the lower part of which evolved the short kilt or
feile-beg, which was more suited to manual labour.

Sir William Wallace (1276-1305), according to
the minstrel, Blind Harry, writing about 1488, wore
an "Ersche mantill," at Dundee. The description
means Highland (Irish or Gaelic). Several writers
of the following century describe the dress of the
Gaels. John Major, the historian, wrote in 1521 of
the wild Scots having no covering for the leg from
the middle of the thigh to the foot, and wearing
mantles.

Breacan-feile, back view,
with targe hung on
shoulder.

Official accounts of 1538 prove that James II. was preparing for a
visit to the Highlands, when he ordered a short "Heland" jacket of
velvet, and tartan hose (stocking trews). A French visitor of 1549
wrote: "they wear no clothes except their dyed shirts and a light
woollen covering of several colours." The material of those days was
much lighter than that produced by power-looms. Old "hard" tartans,
examples of which can be seen in the Tartans Museum at Comrie, were
woven from yarn spun at home by the women, and coloured with vegetable
dyes.

George Buchanan (1506-82), the Latinist, wrote of the Highlanders:
"They delight in variegated garments, especially stripes, and their
favourite colours are purple and blue." An Irish account describes
Hebridean levies sent to Ulster in 1594, as having exterior dress of
"mottled cloaks of many colours, with a fringe to their shins and
calves; their belts were over their loins outside their cloaks." This
is an early reference to the belted plaid or *feileadh mor* ("big
wrap").

Highland dress is represented in Gordon of Rothiemay's map of
Aberdeen, 1661, where he describes the garment as "folded all round

the body about the region of the belt." When the belted plaid was separated in the *feile-beg* and mantle is uncertain, but among the lower ranks of society it was not long after the Jacobite rising of 1715.

The tribal significance of tartans seems to have commenced about the time of the Union of the Crowns, 1603. In 1618, Sir Robert Gordon of Gordonstoun, writing to Murray of Pulrossie, requested him (as a Gordon cadet) "to remove the red and white lines from the plaids of his men, so as to bring them into harmony with other septs."

Undoubtedly the growth of clan tartans owes much to military uniforms. General Wade, Commander of the Forces in Scotland between 1725 and 1740, revived independent companies and ordered the plaids to be near "the same sort and colour." From the dark green tartan chosen evolved the Black Watch sett, variations of which were adopted by several clans.

Tartans came to be worn in the Lowlands after the Union of the Parliaments of Scotland and England in 1707. The detestation of the Union led many people to adopt tartan as a national dress. This is one of Gaeldom's gifts to Scotland.

A vindictive government banned the Highland garb after the '45 Rebellion, but regimental uniforms were excepted. When the Act was repealed in 1782, interest revived. Portraits of Highland chiefs testify to their pride in native costume. It was the visit to Edinburgh in 1822 of George IV, and the guiding hand of Sir Walter Scott, which resulted in a range of new designs, many of them for Lowland families. The fashion was given a further boost through the interest of Queen Victoria and her Consort who purchased the Highland estate of Balmoral for an occasional residence. A Glasgow weaver designed a "Victoria" sett.

Today, there are hundreds of different patterns. Anybody who finds it difficult to justify wearing a clan sett, but has an ancestral connection with areas such as Huntly, Buchan, Strathearn and Lennox, might consider a district tartan. An Edinburgh tartan was designed in 1970. There is also a Jacobite tartan. Advice may be obtained from the Scottish Tartans Society.

8. PRINTED SOURCES

The founding of numerous clan societies in Scotland, from 1725 onwards, overshadowed genealogical studies, which for a long time were confined to the nobility and landed gentry. However, various clubs came into existence and printed material which is of value to genealogists.

A number of gentlemen instituted at Edinburgh in 1822, The Bannatyne Club, named after George Bannatyne (1545-1608), a collector of national poetry. Among the volumes issued to members are **Pitcairn's Criminal Trials**, 1488-1624 (1833); **Baillie's Letters and Journals**, 1637-1662 (1841-42); **Ancient Scottish Seals** (1850); and **The Works of John Knox** (1848-64).

At Glasgow in 1829 was formed The Maitland Club, deriving its name from Sir Richard Maitland (1496-1586), poet and diplomat. **Wodrow's Biographical Collections** was issued 1834-45; **Wodrow's Analecta**, 1842-45; and in 1854 the Club printed **The Caldwell Papers**.

The Spalding Club was inaugurated at Aberdeen in 1841, honouring John Spalding (1609-70), a historian. Among the wealth of material on the north-east printed by the Club are included **The Family Rose of Kilravock**, 1290-1847 (1848); **Fasti Aberdonenses**, 1494-1854 (1854); **List of Pollable Persons, Shire of Aberdeen**, 1696 (1844); **The Family of Skene** (1887); and **History of the Society of Advocates in Aberdeen** (1912). A Supplemental **History of the Society of Advocates** was issued by the Society itself, and covers 1912-1938.

A Scottish Burgh Records Society existed between 1868 and 1910, and printed numerous valuable works, including **Ancient Laws and Customs of the Burghs of Scotland**, 1124-1707, in 2 volumes (1868, 1910); and **Extracts from the Burgh Records of Stirling**, 1625-1747, also in 2 volumes (1871-72).

The early historical clubs were to a large extent superseded by the Scottish History Society, founded in 1887 by the Earl of Rosebery. Among works printed are **MacFarlane's Genealogical Collections**, in 2 volumes (1906-07); **The Scots Brigade in Holland** (1899-1901); **The Scots in Poland**, 1576-1793 (1915); **Forfeited Estates Papers**, 1715, 1745 (1909); and **Prisoners of the '45**, in 3 volumes (1928-29).

In 1897 the Scottish Record Society was founded as a section of the British Records Society, but soon became independent. Almost every volume issued contains genealogical data. Indices to the testament

records in the various commissariots before 1820 were printed in the
early years. Later, prominence was given to printing burgess rolls of
Edinburgh and Glasgow, marriage records, and material related to civil
affairs.

Among the early genealogical writers must be mentioned Alexander
Nisbet (1657-1725), whose **System of Heraldry** was a work of great
labour. The first volume was published in 1722, and the second (with
some unwarranted interpolations) in 1742. The most influential
genealogist of the 18th century was Sir Robert Douglas (1694-1770) of
Glenbervie, whose **Peerage of Scotland,** published 1764, and enlarged by
John P. Wood (1813), formed the foundation of **The Scots Peerage,**
edited by Sir James Balfour Paul, and published in 9 volumes
(1904-14). Sir Robert's **Baronage of Scotland,** 1798, has never been
updated.

It became fashionable in the 19th century for landed families to
have genealogies compiled for private circulation or for inclusion in
Burke's Peerage, or **Burke's Landed Gentry.** The articles in all of
Burkes' publications are listed in an admirable finding aid: **Burke's
Family Index,** by Rosemary Pinches, published at London in 1976.

For information about Scottish clans we recommend **The Clans, Septs
and Regiments of the Scottish Highlands,** by Frank Adam and Sir Thomas
Innes of Learney, and the latter's **Tartans of the Clans and Families
of Scotland,** both in their 8th editions. **The Highland Clans,** by Sir
Iain Moncreiffe, illustrated by David Hicks, is of immense value.
R.W. Munro's **Scottish Clans and Tartans** is the best illustrated book
on the subject. Among the publications in smaller format is **Scottish
Clans and Tartans,** by Ian Grimble.

The following are standard works on armory: **Scots Heraldry,** by Sir
Thomas Innes of Learney, revised (1978) by his son Malcolm R. Innes of
Edingight, and **Simple Heraldry: Cheerfully Illustrated,** by Sir Iain
Moncrieffe and Don Pottinger. The grants and matriculations of arms
from 1672-1902, are described in **An Ordinary of Arms,** by Sir James
Balfour Paul (1903, reprinted Baltimore, 1976). A second volume,
covering 1903-73, by David Reid and Vivian Wilson, was published by
the Lyon Office in 1977.

For the Scottish clergy there is a considerable amount of infor-
mation in print. Those of the Church of Scotland, from the
Reformation to modern times are treated, with genealogical details, in
Fasti Ecclesiae Scoticanae, by Hew Scott. The revised edition,

THE
SCOTS PEERAGE

FOUNDED ON WOOD'S EDITION
OF SIR ROBERT DOUGLAS'S
Peerage of Scotland

CONTAINING

AN HISTORICAL AND GENEALOGICAL ACCOUNT
OF THE NOBILITY OF THAT KINGDOM

EDITED BY

SIR JAMES BALFOUR PAUL
LORD LYON KING OF ARMS

WITH ARMORIAL ILLUSTRATIONS

VOLUME I

EDINBURGH: DAVID DOUGLAS
1904

Title page, The Scots Peerage,

1915-28, is in 7 volumes, to which 3 additional volumes have been added, 1951, 1961, and 1981. J.A. Lamb's **Fasti of the United Free Church**, 1900-29, follows the same pattern. **Annals of the Free Church of Scotland**, by William Ewing, in 2 volumes (1914), covers the ministers and their charges from the Disruption of 1843. The most useful work on the old seceding bodies is R. Small's **History of the United Presbyterian Church**, 1733-1900, in 2 volumes (1904). H.A. Escott's **History of Scottish Congregationalism** (1960), lists the ministers. Baptist ministers and probationers are listed in the current **Baptist Handbook**. For the Roman Catholic clergy there is **The Catholic Directory**, from 1831, but for the Episcopalians there is only the bare lists in successive **Year Books**.

Among books dealing with the legal profession are G.W.T. Ormond's **The Lord Advocates of Scotland**, published in 2 volumes in 1883; Brunton and Haigs' **Senators of the College of Justice** (1832); **The Faculty of Advocates in Scotland**, 1532-1943, printed by the Scottish Record Society in 1944; and **History of the Writers to H.M. Signet**, recently updated. Members of the Faculty of Procurators in Glasgow from 1668 to 1758, are appended to **The Old Minute Book**, printed in 1948.

Graduates and students of Scottish universities have not been accorded the attention they merit, with the exception of those of Aberdeen. **Fasti Academiae Mariscallanae Aberdonensis**, 1593-1860, was printed in 3 volumes by the Spalding Club, 1889-98, and **Officers and Graduates of King's College**, in 1893. There are 4 volumes covering Aberdeen graduates from 1860 to 1970. Glasgow has fared quite well. Apart from **Muniments of the University**, down to 1727, printed by The Maitland Club in 1854, there is a **Roll of Graduates**, 1727-1897, and the **Matriculation Albums**, 1728-1858, a remarkable work, both compiled by W. Ines Addison (1898 and 1913). For St. Andrews, **Acta Facultatis Artium Universitatis Sanctiandree**, 1413-1588, edited by Annie I. Dunlop, was printed by the Scottish History Society in 1964. The same organisation printed in 1926, **Early Records**, containing graduation rolls, 1413-1597, and matriculations, 1473-1579. There is also the **Matriculation Roll**, 1747-1897, published in 1905. For Edinburgh there is only a **Roll of Graduates in Arts, Divinity and Law**, 1587-1858, another for 1859-1888, and a list of **Medical Graduates**, 1705-1845. For the period before Scotland had her own universities there is D.E.R. Watt's scholarly **Biographical Dictionary of Scottish Graduates to A.D. 1410** (1977).

Information about Scottish places is abundant in F.H. Groome's **Gazetteer of Scotland**, of which there are editions from 1882 to 1901 still available in antiquarian bookshops. Places can also be identified with the aid of **Johnston's Gazetteer of Scotland**, revised by R.W. Munro (1973). Among other aids are copies of the **County Directory of Scotland**, up to 1912, and Slater's **Royal National Directory**, various editions from 1862 to 1912. Charles McCaffray's **Index to Sheriff Court Districts in Scotland** (1980), has an alphabetical index of cities, towns and villages.

There are numerous books dealing with surnames, but the standard work is George F. Black's **Surnames of Scotland** (New York, 1946), reprinted. P.H. Reaney's book, **A Dictionary of British Surnames**, is authoritative, and gives surviving spellings as well as referenced examples from the earliest times.

Ulster-Scots are treated in Charles A. Hanna's **The Scotch-Irish**, published in 1902, and reprinted at Baltimore in 1968. Among more recent studies are: **Ulster Emigration to Colonial America**, 1718–1775, by R.J. Dickson (1966); **Essays in Scotch-Irish History**, by E.R.R. Green (1969); and **The Scottish Migration to Ulster in the Reign of James I.**, by M. Perceval-Maxwell (1973). There is also **Scotch Irish Research Made Simple**, by R.G. Campbell (Munroe Falls, 1980).

For advanced students of Scottish genealogy we recommend Gerald Hamilton-Edward's **In Search of Scottish Ancestry**, now in its 2nd edition. D.J. Steel's **Sources for Scottish Genealogy and Family History** (1970) is useful. **The Sources of Scottish History**, by Professor Gordon Donaldson (1978), is of value to genealogists as well as indispensable to historians.

Printed family histories are listed in Margaret Stuart's **Scottish Family History** (1930), and in Joan P.S. Ferguson's **Scottish Family Histories held in Scottish Libraries** (1960), both of which have been reprinted.

9. THE EMIGRANT SCOT

Long before the colonisation of the New World, Scotland sent many of her sons to Europe, Scandinavia and Ireland. They were thought of as "Scots overseas," rather than emigrants, and a proportion of them returned home after spending their working lives abroad. Others settled permanently in Sweden, Russia, Poland, Germany, France and Holland.

So far as North America is concerned, it was not ignorance which held back the Scots. As early as 1597/98, the Town Council of Aberdeen received from Robert Lyndsey, a pilot, the gift of "the haill universall see kart of Europ, Affrica and Asaia, and new found lands of America." It was probably long after this event before any Aberdeen shipmaster braved the storms of the Atlantic.

England resented the Scottish presence on the high seas; and to add to the difficulties, there was piracy, to which all nations turned a blind eye. Centuries before the Plantation of Ulster, the surplus menfolk of the West Highlands and Islands found homes in Northern Ireland. It was, however, the flight to Europe of Irish chiefs desperate to avoid charges of treason, that left King James with large tracts of land in Ulster. The Plantation by Scots and English Protestants was put into effect about 1610. All the grantees undertook to live in Ulster and to take with them 48 able men. Wives went too, hence the propagation of the people known as Ulster-Scots, many of whom emigrated to America. The term "Scotch-Irish" is a misnomer, implying a mixture of nations which is belied by the facts.

Scotland's earliest attempt at colonisation was conceived by the same monarch; but it fell to his son Charles to attempt the settlement of Nova Scotia (New Scotland), on the seaboard of North America. The interest of the King was expressed in a letter to the Privy Council in Scotland, directing them to grant to Sir William Alexander of Menstrie, his heirs and assignees, and any who would join him, a signature under the Great Seal of the Royal Province of Nova Scotia. This was followed in 1621 by a charter, now in the Royal Ontario Museum, of lands covering some 36,000 square miles of land in Nova Scotia and New Brunswick.

Progress was disappointing. Despite the creation of an order of Baronets of Nova Scotia, with an obligation to furnish men, only small settlements were made at Port Royal (Annapolis) and Baleine Harbour. The colony was abandoned when the French right to Acadia was recognised in 1632. Later, Nova Scotia attracted thousands of Scots.

Scotland's other attempt at Colonisation--The Darien Scheme--was intended to form an emporium on either side of the Isthmus of Panama, and so secure the trade of opposite continents. In two groups, some 2,500 people sailed for Panama in 1698 and 1699, and a settlement was made. The leaders knew little of colonisation, and the provisions were unsuited to the climate or soon exhausted. The groups lacked co-ordination, and famine and disease took their toll. Moreover, the Spaniards were hostile, and it was decided to abandon the scheme. Nearly 2,000 colonists were buried in Panama, drowned in the Caribbean, or rotted in Spanish prisons. Nine ships were lost and only about 30 Scots returned home. The other survivors sought refuge in English colonies. It was a catastropic curtain to the last act of Scotland's independence.

At the time of the Darien disaster, there were small Scottish settlements on the Potomac and in New Hampshire, and merchant colonies in Virginia. Throughout the 17th century there had been a steady trickle of emigrants from Scotland to America and the West Indies, enlarged by Royalist prisoners sent out by Cromwell in 1651, and later by Covenanters. The "hotch-potch" Scottish-Quaker-Catholic-Covenanter 24 proprietors of East New Jersey attracted settlers, and from institutions such as the 'Log College' and Princeton there radiated influences traceable to Ulster and the Scottish Lowlands.

The first half of the 18th century was marked by the deportation of Jacobite prisoners, those who had supported the Stuarts against the Hanovarian government. The Rebellion of 1715 was a model of mismanagement and resulted in the transportation of about 700 prisoners. The Rebellion of 1745 was more serious, but the hopes of Prince Charles Edward Stuart ended at Culloden Moor. More than 900 prisoners were transported after the battle.

From 1730 onwards, military service provided an outlet for the surplus menfolk of the Highlands. Scottish regiments served in North America during the Seven Years War, and discharged soldiers were encouraged to settle. Those who returned home stimulated further emigration. Agricultural improvement was being promoted, and Highland tacksmen, whose mode of life had changed since the '45, were emigrating with many of their sub-tenants. One of the earliest Scottish settlements was in Georgia, and there were others in North Carolina and New York.

Around 1770 there was emigration from ports in the north and northwest, while other Highlanders tramped to Greenock to join Renfrewshire weavers affected by the introduction of the power-loom, and other Lowlanders ruined by the failure of the Ayr bank of Douglas and Heron. It was at this time that emigration to the maritime provinces of Canada commenced.

After the thirteen original colonies had passed forever from British control, thousands of Loyalists left for Canada. This was really the birth of Upper Canada or Ontario. Other settlements were made in the provinces of Quebec, New Brunswick and Nova Scotia. A large number who found the principles of the Revolution to their liking, remained to make contributions to the civilisation of the United States. The War of 1812 also had the effect of slowing down the flow of emigrants and transferring interest to Canada.

Numerous Scots distinguished themselves in their adopted country. During the colonial period some 30 provincial governors were Scots. At least 11 of George Washington's successors were of Scots or Ulster-Scots extraction: Monroe, Grant, Hayes, Theodore Roosevelt, Wilson, Polk, Buchanan, Arthur, McKinley, Jackson and Johnson.   At least six Vice-Presidents and more than 150 cabinet ministers had Scottish blood.   The financial ability--perhaps the frugality--of the race has been recognised, and about half of the Secretaries of the Treasury could be named as of Scottish descent; moreover, nearly a third of the Secretaries of State.

Scottish settlements in the maritime provinces of Canada were augmented by discharged soldiers who received grants of land in Nova Scotia after the Revolution. The notorious Highland Clearances also resulted in the movement of people from the Highlands and Western Isles to Canada.

For centuries the mountainous districts of Scotland had supported only wildlife.   The Highland cattle were unfit for grazing on the steep declivities, and the domestic sheep were so frail they were folded or housed at night.   The landlords realised that sheep of an improved breed could forage all the year round on the mountains as they had done for ages on the Border hills, and the Cheviot breed was introduced about 1768.   They were not extensively adopted until the beginning of the next century.   In some areas landowners extended the sheepwalks into the populated glens and changed the primitive system of agriculture without any sense of communal responsibility.   Deer and grouse estates came later.

There were many Scots in Lower Canada before the territory was ceded to Britain.   When Wolfe beseiged Quebec he found Franco-Scots and exiled Jacobites among the defenders. The fur trade had brought Orkneymen to the Hudson's Bay Company, and others--mainly Highlanders--made Montreal their center for trapping excursions in the north-west.

Many Scots took part in explorations. Alexander Mackenzie made his historic journeys to the Artic Sea (1789) and Pacific Coast (1792-93) while representing the North-West Company. Among many others was Simon Fraser, whose epic voyage down the river which bears his name virtually commenced British Columbia's association with Canada.

Lord Selkirk launched a prosperous colonisation scheme on Prince Edward Island in 1803, and the following year a disastrous programme at Baldoon, in Kent County, Ontario. His next venture was to settle Highlanders on a large tract of land on the Red River. The scheme was opposed by the North-West Company, and there was much trouble before their fur-traders merged with the Hudson's Bay Company in 1821. The way was now open for farming on the prairies, and the great company transferred vast territorities to the Government in 1869, just two years after Confederation was born in the east.

Scots have played a leading role in the mapping of Canada; in education, commerce and politics. Perhaps their greatest achievement--aided by the political skills of John A. MacDonald--was to bring British Columbia into the Confederation by projecting the Canadian-Pacific Railroad and making Canada a transcontinental nation.

The American Revolution not only speeded up the settlement of Canada, but terminated the system of transporting convicts and political prisoners to North America. This forced the British Government to look elsewhere, and the answer came from Joseph Banks, who proposed Botany Bay, in Australia. So, in a curious way, the subsequent colonisation of the sub-continent and New Zealand started with the first clash of arms at Lexington in 1775.

APPENDIX D.

Page 24.—LIST OF RED RIVER SETTLERS OF 1812-1814.

(Taken from Transaction No. 33 of the Historical and Scientific Society of Manitoba.)

List of men belonging to the Red River Settlement, arriving in Hudson Bay in 1811, and brought from York Factory, July, 1812—

Colin Campbell, aged 21, from Argyle, labourer.
John McKay, aged 22, from Ross-shire, boatbuilder.
John McLennan, aged 23, from Ross-shire, labourer.
Beth Bethune, aged 19, from Ross-shire, labourer.
Donald McKay, aged 17, from Ross-shire, labourer.
William Wallace, aged 21, from Ayr, labourer.
John Cooper, aged 26, from Orkney, labourer.
Nieill Harper, aged 34, from Orkney, labourer.
Magnus Isbister, aged 21, from Orkney, labourer.
Geo. Gibbon, aged 50, from Orkney, labourer.
Thos. McKim, aged 38, from Sligo, overseer.
Pat. Corcoran, aged 24, from Crossmilina, carpenter.
John Green, aged 21, from Sligo, labourer.
Pat. Quinn, aged 21, from Killalla, labourer.
Martin Jordan, aged 16, from Killalla, labourer.
John O'Rourke, aged 20, from Killalla, labourer.
Anthony McDonnell, aged 23, from Killalla, labourer.
James Toomey, aged 20, from Sligo, labourer.
18 in all.

LIST OF SETTLERS WHO LANDED AT CHURCHILL IN AUGUST, 1813, AND PROCEEDING OVERLAND TO YORK FACTORY, ARRIVED IN THE SPRING OF 1814 AT RED RIVER.

Passengers on board the *Prince of Wales* for Red River Settlement—

1. Geo. Campbell, aged 25, from Archwigle Parish, Creech, Sutherland.
2. Helen, his wife, aged 20.
3. Bell, his daughter, aged 1.
4. John Sutherland, aged 50, from Kildonan. Died 2nd September at C. F., a very respectable man.
5. Catherine, his wife, aged 46.
6. George, his son, aged 18.
7. Donald, his son, aged 16.

8. Alexander, his son, aged 9.
9. Jannet, his daughter, aged 14.
10. Angus McKay, aged 24, from Kildonan.
11. Jean, his wife.
12. Alex. Gunn, aged 50, from Kildonan.
13. Christina, his wife, aged 50. Died 20th September, C. F.
14. William, his son, aged 18.
15. Donald Bannerman, aged 50. Died 24th September at C. F.
16. Christina, his wife, aged 44.
17. William, his son, aged 18.
18. Donald, his son, aged 8.
19. Christina, his daughter, aged 16.
20. Geo. McDonald, aged 48. Died 1st September, 1813, C. F.
21. Jannet, his wife, aged 50.
22. Betty Grey, aged 17.
23. Catherine Grey, aged 23.
24. Barbara McBeath, widow, aged 45, Borobal.
25. Charles, her son, aged 16.
26. Jenny (her daughter), aged 23.
27. Andrew McBeath, aged 19.
28. Jannet, his wife.
29. William Sutherland, aged 22, from Borobal.
30. Margaret, his wife, aged 15.
31. Christina, his sister, aged 24.
32. Donald Gunn, aged 63, from Borobal.
33. Jannet, his wife, aged 50.
34. (Transferred to the *Eddystone*, for H. B. Co. service.)
35. Geo. Gunn, son to Donald, aged 16, from Borobal, Parish Kildonan.
36. Esther, his daughter, aged 24.
37. Catherine, his daughter, aged 20. Died 29th August, 1813, C. F.
38. Christian, his daughter, aged 10.
39. Angus Gunn, aged 21.
40. Jannet, his wife.
41. Robert Sutherland, brother to William. No. 29, aged 17, from Borobal.
42. Elizabeth Fraser, sister to No. 30, aged 30.
43. Angus Sutherland, aged 20, from Auchraluie.
44. Elizabeth, his mother, aged 60.
45. Betsy, his sister, aged 18. Died of consumption.
46. Donald Stewart, from Parish of Appin. Died 20th August, 1813, at C. F.
47. Catherine, his wife, aged 30.
48. Margaret, his daughter, aged 8.
49. Mary, his daughter, aged 5.
50. Ann, his daughter, aged 2.
51. John Smith, from Parish Kildonan.
52. Mary, his wife.
53. John, his son.
54. Jean, his daughter.
55. Mary, his daughter.
56. Alex. Gunn, aged 58, from Parish of Kildonan, Sutherland.
57. Elizabeth McKay, his niece.
58. Betsy McKay, his niece.

'Selkirk settlers,' from Archer Martin's *Hudson Bay Company's Land Tenures* (London, 1898).

10. ADDRESS LIST

SCOTLAND

Archives: National

Episcopal Church in Scotland
The Theological College,
Rosebery Crescent,
EDINBURGH, EH12 25JT

General Register Office,
(Registrar General for Scotland),
New Register House,
EDINBURGH, EH1 3YT

Scottish Catholic Archives,
Columba House,
16 Drummond Place,
EDINBURGH, EH3 6PL

Scottish Record Office
H.M. General Register House,
Princes Street,
EDINBURGH, EH1 3YY

Archives: Regional

Borders -
Bridge Street,
HAWICK, TD9 9QT

Highland -
Highland Regional Council
The Castle, INVERNESS

Central -
Spittal Street,
STIRLING, FK8 1DY

Lothian -
Edinburgh City Archives,
City Chambers,
EDINBURGH, EH1 1YT

Dumfries & Galloway -
Ewart Library,
Catherine Street,
DUMFRIES, DG1 1JB

Orkney & Shetland -
The Orkney Library,
Laing Street,
KIRKWALL, Orkney Islands

Lothian -
Edinburgh City Archives,
City Chambers,
EDINBURGH, EH1 1YJ

Strathclyde -
P.O. Box 27,
City Chambers,
GLASGOW, G2 1DU

Fife -
Dunfermline Libraries,
1 Abbot Street,
DUNFERMLINE, KY12 7NL

Tayside -
Archive & Record Centre,
14 City Square,
DUNDEE, DD1 1DB

Grampian –
Woodhill House,
Ashgrove Road West,
ABERDEEN, AB9 2LU

Western Isles –
Public Library,
STORNOWAY, Isle of Lewis

Educational

Centre for Scottish Studies,
Taylor Buildings,
King's College,
OLD ABERDEEN, AB9 2UB

School of Scottish Studies,
27 George Square,
EDINBURGH, EH8 9LD

Centre of Canadian Studies,
University of Edinburgh,
21 George Square,
EDINBURGH, EH8 9LD

The Heritage of Scotland,
International Summer Schools,
University of Stirling,
STIRLING, FK9 4LA

Genealogical/Historical

Aberdeen & North-East Scotland
Family History Society,
31 Bloomfield Place,
ABERDEEN, AB1 5AG

Scottish Genealogy Society,
9 Union Street,
EDINBURGH, EH1 3LT

Court of the Lord Lyon,
New Register House,
EDINBURGH, EH1 3YT

Scottish History Society,
Department of History,
University of Aberdeen,
ABERDEEN, AB9 2UB

Glasgow & West of Scotland
Family History Society,
5 Laburnum Grove,
Kirkintilloch,
GLASGOW, G66 4DF

Scottish Records Association,
University Library,
DUNDEE, DD1 4HN

Heraldry Society of Scotland,
c/o Society of Antiquaries
   of Scotland,
Queen Street, Edinburgh, EH2 1JD

Scottish Record Society,
Department of Scottish History,
University of Glasgow,
GLASGOW, G12 8QH

Highland Family History Society,
53 Balifeary Road,
INVERNESS, 1V3

Scots Ancestry Research Society,
3 Albany Street,
EDINBURGH, EH1 3PY

Society of Antiquaries of
   Scotland,
National Museum of Antiquities,
Queen Street,
EDINBURGH, EH2 1JD

Tay Valley Family History Society,
II Turfbeg Road, Forfar,
ANGUS, DD1 3EX

Society of West Highland & Island
Historical Research,
Breacachadh Castle,
Isle of Coll, ARGYLL, PA78 6TB

Society of Heraldry & Genealogy
St. Salvator's Hall,
University of St. Andrews,
St. ANDREWS, Fife,
or
9 Priestden Park,
St. ANDREWS, KY16 8DL

Libraries

North-East Scotland Library
   Services,
14 Crown Terrace,
ABERDEEN, AB9 2BH

The Mitchell Library,
North Street
GLASGOW, G3t7DN

National Library of Scotland,
George IV. Bridge,
EDINBURGH, EH1 1EW

William Coull Anderson
Library of Genealogy,
Dewar House, Hill Terrace,
ARBROATH, Angus, DD11 1AJ

Social/Cultural

An Commun Gaidhealach,
Abertarff House, Church Street,
INVERNESS, IV1 1EU

The Saltire Society,
13 Atholl Crescent,
EDINBURGH, EH3 8HA

Research Centre,
Museum of Scottish Tartans,
Scottish Tartans Society,
COMRIE, Perthshire, PH6 2DW

The St. Andrew Society,
P.O. Box 84,
Edinburgh,

National Museum of Antiquities,
   and also Scottish National
   Portrait Gallery,
1 Queen Street,
EDINBURGH, EH2 1JD

The Scottish Tourist Board,
23 Ravelston Terrace,
EDINBURGH, EH4 3EU
Also c/o British Tourist Authority,
680 Fifth Avenue, New York,
N.Y., 10019

National Trust for Scotland,   The Standing Council of Scottish
5 Charlotte Square,   Chiefs,
EDINBURGH, EH2 4DU   12 Hope Street,
                              EDINBURGH, EH2 4DO

Scots and people of Scots descent in various countries should con-
sult **World Directory of Scottish Associations,** compiled and edited
by Michael Brander and Iseabail Macleod (Edinburgh & London, 1979).
There are sections relating to Great Britain and Ireland, The Ameri-
cas, Australasia and the Far East, Africa and the Middle East, and
Europe.   North American residents would also find **The Claymore:
Newsletter of Scottish Information and Services,** published by the
Council of Scottish Clan Associations, of value.   Their address is:

Secretary, 711 Chateau Apartments, Carrboro, NC   27510.

NORTH AMERICA

American-Scottish Foundation,   The Augustan Society,
Scotland House,   1510 Cravens Ave.,
124 East 29th Street,   TORRANCE, CA   90501
NEW YORK, NY, 10001

Canadian Association of   The National Archives &
   Scottish Studies,   Records Service,
c/o McLaughlin Library,   General Services Administration,
University of Guelph,   WASHINGTON   25, D.C.
GUELPH, Ont., N1G ZW1

Clans & Scottish Societies   The Scots-Irish Society of
   of Canada   the U.S.A.,
95 Laurel Ave.,   205 Lansdowne Road,
ISLINGTON, Ont., M9B 4T1   HAVERTOWN, PA 19083

Dacus Library   Ontario Genealogical Society,
Scottish Archives   Box 66, Station Q,
Winthrop College   TORONTO, Ont., M4T 2LT
Rock Hill, SC   29733

Genealogical Association of the
Royal Nova Scotia Historical
Society,
P.O. Box 641, Station M,
HALIFAX, NS, B3J 2T3

Genealogical Library,
(British Reference),
50 E. North Temple Street,
SALT LAKE CITY, UT 84150

Institute of Scottish Studies,
Old Dominion University,
NORFOLK, VA 23508

International Society for British
Genealogy and Family History,
P.O. Box 20425,
CLEVELAND, OH 44125

Library of Congress,
WASHINGTON, D.C., 20540

New England Historic Genealogical
Society,
101 Newbury Street
BOSTON, MA 02116

New York Public Library,
Fifth Avenue at 42nd Street,
NEW YORK, NY 10018

Public Archives of Canada,
395 Wellington,
OTTAWA, Ont., K1A 0N3

Public Archives of Nova Scotia,
6016 University Ave.,
HALIFAX, NS, B3H 1W4

Scottish Historic & Research
Society of the Delaware Valley,
102 St. Paul's Road,
ARDMORE, PA 19003

Scottish Heritage Foundation,
9621 Campo Road,
SPRING VALLEY, CA 92027

Scottish Lowland Clans and
Family Society of
North America
35 S. Encino Road,
SOUTH LAGUNA, CA 92677

The Western Reserve
Historical Society,
Genealogical Committee,
10825 East Boulevard,
CLEVELAND, OH 44106

AUSTRALASIA

Armorial & Genealogical Institute
of New Zealand,
P.O. Box 13301, Armagh,
CHRISTCHURCH, NZ

South Australian Genealogy
& Heraldry Society, Inc.,
P.O. Box 13,
Marsden, 5070,
SOUTH AUSTRALIA

National Library of Australia,
  Canberra, ACT 2600
AUSTRALIA

New Zealand Society of
  Genealogists,
P.O. Box 8795,
AUCKLAND 4, NZ

Queensland Family History Society,
P.O. Box 171,
Indooroopilly, Brisbane,
Queensland, 4068,
AUSTRALIA

Western Australia
Genealogical Society,
P.O. Box 7, West Perth,
WESTERN AUSTRALIA, 6005

Society of Australian Genealogists,
120 Kent Street, Observatory Hill,
Sydney, NSW 200, AUSTRALIA

SCOTTISH RESEARCH

It is advisable when engaging a professional researcher for work in Scotland to choose a Member of the Association of Scottish Genealogists and Record Agents, who work to a strict Code of Practice. Some members are consultants and not available for private commissions, but those who accept assignments are listed here in alphabetical arrangement:

Mrs. A.R. Bigwood, M.A., M.Litt.,
38 Primrose Bank,
EDINBURGH, EH5 3JF

Mrs. Sheila Pitcairn, L.H.G.
Honorary Secretary, A.S.G.R.A.,
106 Brucefield Ave.,
DUNFERMLINE, Fife, KY11 4SY

Mrs. Doreen Brown,
64 Orchard Road,
EDINBURGH, EH4 2HD

Miss F. Lloyd Pritchard, Ph.D.,
36 Morton Street, Joppa,
EDINBURGH, EH15 2HT

Mr. David G.C. Burns,
2 Bangholm Terrace,
EDINBURGH, EH3 5QN

Mrs. Daniella Shippey, M.A.,
15 Glenisla Gardens,
EDINBURGH, EH9 2HR

Mrs. Betty Iggo, Ph.D.,
5 Relugas Road,
EDINBURGH, EH9 2NE

Mrs. Margaret Sinclair,
83 Newington Road,
EDINBURGH, EH9 2HR

Mrs. Gwen MacLeod, F.S.A.Scot.,   Mr. James A. Thomson,
5 Bonaly Road,   84 Gilmore Place,
EDINBURGH, EH13 0EB   EDINBURGH, EH3 9PF

Fees will depend on the extent and the nature of the work. Those wishing to have research carried out should send a preliminary letter indicating what is required, and giving any information which would assist the searcher. Association members can provide an assessment of probable costs, or work to limits of time and expenditure. A stamped and addressed envelope (if overseas, International Reply Coupons) should be sent with the inquiry.

REGIMENTAL HEADQUARTERS

The Royal Scots, The Castle, Edinburgh.
The Royal Highland Fusiliers, 518 Sauchiehall Street, Glasgow.
The King's Own Scottish Borders, The Barracks, Berwick-on-Tweed.
The Cameronians, 129 Muir Street, Hamilton, Lanarkshire.
The Black Watch, Balhousie Castle, Perth.
The Queen's Own Highlanders, Cameron Barracks, Inverness.
The Gordon Highlanders, Viewfield Road, Aberdeen.
The Argyll & Sutherland Highlanders, The Castle, Stirling.